KT-167-651

Essential
Budapest

by Rob Stuart

Rob Stuart divides his time between
television work and travel writing. He has a
special interest in adventure travel, and his
articles have appeared in various national
newspapers, including the *Telegraph*, the
Guardian and the *Independent*. Two of his
river expeditions appeared in the AA's
Great Voyages of the World (1997).

Above: *the Danube from Castle Hill*

AA Publishing

*A host of excellent local
wines awaits the visitor*

**Written by Rob Stuart
Updated by Bob Dent**

Published and distributed in the United Kingdom by AA
Publishing, a trading name of Automobile Association
Developments Limited, whose registered office is Norfolk
House, Priestley Road, Basingstoke, Hampshire, RG24 9NY.
Registered number 1878835.

© Automobile Association Developments Limited 1998,
2001
Maps © Automobile Association Developments Limited
1998, 2001
Reprinted 2001. Information verified and updated.

A CIP catalogue record for this book is available from the
British Library.

ISBN 0 7495 1904 5

The contents of this publication are believed correct at
the time of printing. Nevertheless, the publishers cannot
be held responsible for any errors or omissions or for
changes in the details given in this guide or for the
consequences of any reliance on the information provided
by the same. Assessments of attractions, hotels,
restaurants and so forth are based upon the author's own
experience and, therefore, descriptions given in this guide
necessarily contain an element of subjective opinion which
may not reflect the publisher's opinion or dictate a reader's
own experience on another occasion.

We have tried to ensure accuracy in this guide, but
things do change and we would be grateful if readers
would advise us of any inaccuracies they may encounter.

Find out more about
AA Publishing and the
wide range of services
the AA provides by
visiting our web site at
www.theAA.com

Colour separation: BTB Digital Imaging, Whitchurch,
Hampshire
Printed and bound in Italy by Printers Trento S.r.l.

Contents

About this Book

Essential Budapest is divided into five sections to cover the most important aspects of your visit to Budapest.

Viewing Budapest pages 5–14
An introduction to Budapest by the author.
Budapest's Features
Essence of Budapest
The Shaping of Budapest
Peace and Quiet
Budapest's Famous

Top Ten pages 15–26
The author's choice of the Top Ten places to see in Budapest, listed in alphabetical order, each with practical information.

What to See pages 27–90
The two main areas of Budapest and excursions from the city, each with its own brief introduction and an alphabetical listing of the main attractions
Practical information
Snippets of 'Did You Know...' information
4 suggested walks
2 suggested tours
2 features

Where To... pages 91–116
Detailed listings of the best places to eat, stay, shop, take the children and be entertained.

Practical Matters pages 117–24
A highly visual section containing essential travel information.

Maps
All map references are to the individual maps found in the What to See section of this guide.
For example, Budavári Palota (Buda Castle Palace) has the reference ✚ 29C3 – indicating the page on which the map is located and the grid square in which the palace is to be found. A list of the maps that have been used in this travel guide can be found in the index.

Prices
Where appropriate, an indication of the cost of an establishment is given by **£** signs:
£££ denotes higher prices, **££** denotes average prices, while **£** denotes lower charges.

Star Ratings
Most of the places described in this book have been given a separate rating:

✪✪✪ Do not miss
✪✪ Highly recommended
✪ Worth seeing

Viewing
Budapest

Above: *rustic street lamp*
Right: *one of many statues
in Heroes' Square*

Rob Stuart's Budapest

Changing Mentality
The transition from mild totalitarianism to market economy in the last few years has had a considerable impact on the Hungarian people. While the new liberal policies are generally welcome, nevertheless there's a lingering nostalgia, particularly among the older folk, for the stability and security of the old regime. Budapest itself in recent times has become more contemporary, more sophisticated, more commercially oriented, more individualistic in attitude, but also (some observe) more segregated, more scandal-ridden, more commonplace. Alongside the economic optimism, there is a sense of gloom, even disillusionment.

Over dinner of pike in creamy dill sauce (which goes to show how inventive Hungarian cuisine is), and accompanied by our second bottle of Etyek Sauvignon Blanc, János, a Budapest student, politely rebuked me for repeatedly referring to Budapest and Hungary as Eastern European. 'Hungary is a Middle-European country, or if you prefer, Central European,' he emphasised. He was right to correct me. Geographically, Hungary is at the very centre of Europe, and Budapest, its capital, at its very heart.

The term Middle Europe has of course dark historical associations. Centuries of turbulence and upheaval, of war and revolution – in the case of Hungary, from the Magyar Conquest to the 1956 Uprising – have left their indelible mark on Budapest. A city of solemn, heroic beauty – Buda, the historical half of the city on the west bank of the River Danube, and Pest (pronounced 'pesht'), the commercial half on the east bank – Budapest stands as splendid testament to Hungary's unvanquishable spirit, as well as to the pride, courage and resourcefulness of its people.

Like the Danube that sweeps majestically down to the Black Sea, the city itself sweeps the visitor along. Vibrant, frenetic, gentle, but never dull, Budapest's appeal is its blend of cosmopolitanism and patrician elegance, of dynamism and parochial tranquillity. And, like all capital cities of reputation, it caters for every taste, from high culture to marathon vodka sessions.

Budapest is not a city to be approached timidly. Its grandeur, size, pace and diversity of life may seem overwhelming and even formidable at times, but that's all part of the Budapest 'experience.' And it is indeed just that – an experience.

Vajdahunyad Castle, a fairy-tale treat in Budapest's City Park

Budapest's Features

Geography

• Hungary occupies the Carpathian Basin, a vast plain at the centre of Eastern Europe. The River Danube divides Hungary's 93,030sq km into the Great Plain, the puszta, on the east and Transdanubia (Nagyalföld) on the west. The Great Plain is, in size and appearance, reminiscent of the Ukrainian steppes and the American prairie. Hungary's 'mountains' are little more than hills, seldom exceeding 1,000m in height. The highest peak is Kékes (1,014m) in the Mátra range northeast of Budapest. Much of Hungary is less than 200m above sea level. Lake Balaton, southwest of Budapest, is the largest freshwater lake in Europe.

Economy

• Budapest is the commercial and industrial heart of Hungary. A burgeoning service sector, partly the result of booming tourism, is a major employer, though traditional manufacturing industries such as textiles, chemicals, iron and steel, also employ a significant part of the population. With the advent of the free-market economy, Hungary has attracted substantial foreign investment, most noticeably in the sectors of car assembly, high-tech electronics, and light manufacturing.

Summertime, when café life spills on to the streets

Language

• Magyar, the language of Hungary, is part of the Finno-Ugric language group, distantly related to Finnish, as well as to about a dozen or so other minor languages in Russia and western Siberia. It is a difficult language at which a guess can lead to real confusion. German, which up untill now has been Hungarians' second language, is now being overtaken by English, especially among the young.

Climate

• Budapest experiences a temperate continental climate characterised by cold winters (the average temperature drops to -2°C) and hot summers, when the average temperature rises to 22°C, but expect much higher temperatures (around 30°C) and be prepared for oppressive humidity, especially in August.

Essence of Budapest

Straddling the Danube with its nine bridges, Budapest has a bewildering array of architectural styles, a legacy of its turbulent history. Neo-classical, neo-Gothic, neo-Renaissance are just a few, and help create a skyline of astonishing grandeur. Budapest is not just a capital city, it is also a city of empire. Its soubriquet 'Queen of the Danube' is rightly deserved. But make no mistake – far from being regally remote and austere, this 'queen' dresses rather chicly, is modishly cosmopolitan, and is inclined to drive in the fast lane. To adapt a quotation: 'when you're tired of Budapest, you're tired of life.'

Below: *the city straddles the broad River Danube*
Inset: *an organ-grinder brings music to the streets*

THE **10** ESSENTIALS

If you only have a short time to visit Budapest, or would like to get a really complete picture of the city, here are the essentials:

- **Stand atop Gellért-hegy (Gellért Hill)** for spectacular views of the city, as well as the Citadella, a fortress of white stone (➤ 18–19).
- **Muse, or be amused, by** Halászbástya (Fishermen's Bastion), an architectural fantasy that wouldn't look out of place on a Disney set (➤ 19).
- **Admire Mátyás-templom (Matthias Church)** in all its neo-Gothic magnificence in Trinity Square.
- **Wander the picturesque streets** of Várhegy (Castle Hill), or just soak up the atmosphere at one of the many bars and cafés there (➤ 26).
- **Visit the Budavári Palota (Royal Palace)** and the several museums in its confines (➤ 16).
- **Stroll down Andrássy út**, at one time the most fashionable promenading route in Budapest (➤ 56).
- **Take a relaxing dip** in one of the many gyógyfürdö (thermal baths) if foot-sore from trudging the streets.

- **Visit Vörösmarty tér,** a pedestrianised and peaceful square, but only after you've browsed the most exclusive shopping street Váci utca (➤ 77).
- **Marvel at the architectural** magnificence of Országház, the parliament building – you could almost be in London (➤ 23).
- **Take refuge from the hustle of the city** on peaceful Margit-sziget (Margaret Island) in the middle of the Danube (➤ 21).

Budapest is a city of parks and grand architectural design

The Shaping of Budapest

Roman remains of Budapest's ancient past

6th century BC
The Eravisci, a Celtic tribe of craftsmen, settle on Buda's Gellért Hill.

1st century AD
Aquincum (now Óbuda) established by Romans.

5th century
The Huns occupy Aquincum after the Romans depart.

896
The Magyars set about conquering the Carpathian Basin.

1000
Christianity officially imposed on the Hungarian nation.

12th century
French and German traders settle in the area of Buda and Pest, as yet still villages.

1241
Pest destroyed by Mongol hordes.

14th and 15th centuries
Buda flourishes during the reigns of Louis I and King-Emperor Sigismund.

15th century
Buda becomes a centre of Renaissance learning.

1541
Buda falls to the Turks.

1686
A combined European force recaptures Buda and Austrian Hapsburg rule begins.

1795
Jacobin conspiracy defeated.

1848
The Chain Bridge built, linking Buda and Pest.

1849
Hungarian forces defeated by combined Russian and Austrian armies.

1867
The Ausgleich, or Compromise, grants a measure of autonomy to Hungary.

1873
Buda and Pest amalgamated.

1896
Millenary celebrations mark the 1,000th anniversary of the Magyar Conquest.

1918
Hungary proclaims itself
an independent republic.

1941
Under Admiral Horthy,
Hungary allies itself with
Germany.

1944
The Germans occupy
Budapest.

1945
Budapest in ruins as the
Soviets take control.

1956
The Hungarian Uprising
sees spirited but
eventually futile
demonstrations against
Soviet Russian tanks as
Hungarians strive for
political reform.

*Ceremonial burning of
Stalin's portrait during the
1956 uprising*

1989
János Kádár, Hungary's
reforming leader for 32
years, dies.

1993
Free-market economy
begins in earnest.

1997
The government
attempts to transfer 80
per cent of the economy
to private ownership.

*Chain Bridge, arguably
the most attractive of all
Budapest's bridges*

11

Peace & Quiet

Budapest, like any major city, can be exhausting for the visitor. With madding crowds, traffic noise and the general hurly-burly of the city, life can sometimes be fretful. Rest assured, Budapest has a plentiful supply of tranquil enclaves, from backstreet cafés and bars to city-centre parks or, further afield, the Buda Hills or the unmissable Royal Danube Bend – an enchanting pastoral idyll just 20 minutes from the city. But don't use these places simply as a refuge from the pressure of city life. Even in the most frantic places in Budapest, the traditionally warm Hungarian hospitality ensures that someone will find you a seat at a bar or café.

Parks and Gardens

Though Budapest has an abundance of parks and gardens, during the summer, on public holidays and weekends, they won't be quite the havens of tranquillity you would wish. Margit-sziget (Margaret Island ➤ 21), though cut off from the city by the Danube and offering woodlands and gardens as well as swimming pools and sports grounds, is a very popular venue for Pestians and tourists alike. However, if all you want is to escape the traffic, this is the place to come. Private vehicles are banned. Városliget (City Park ➤ 74) has extensive gardens and woodland, also a

Leisurely Lake Balaton is just a short trip away from Budapest

zoo, transport and agricultural museums, a circus and baths. Such amenities naturally attract people so don't expect to stroll alone listening to no more than birdsong and the rustle of leaves. Strictly speaking, Budai-hegység (Buda Hills) are neither park nor garden but they are as peaceful a place as you will find so near to the city. Comprising three hills – St John's Hill, the Hill of the Three Boundaries and Freedom Hill – they offer woodland trails, the habitat

of woodpeckers and warblers, and short ski-lifts to allow exploration. Near by, but not necessarily a quiet spot, is Budakeszi Game Park with wild boar and deer.

The golden oriole, one of Budapest's most colourful summer visitors

Wildlife

In and around the city of Budapest the woodlands abound with birdlife, especially in springtime when the resident birds are augmented by huge numbers of migratory birds – the elusive golden oriole, for example, with its distinctive fluty song. Also several species of warblers arrive at this time of year, among them Bonelli's warbler, with its high-pitched trilling song. Less conspicuous but worth looking out for is the honey buzzard, a bird of prey that soars on rounded wings marked with bars. Among the city's commonest birds are the delightful flycatchers: the collared flycatcher with its black-and-white plumage and the red-breasted flycatcher, frenetic on the wing, with a constantly dipping tail.

Further Afield

Many of the best wildlife areas, including national parks and reserves, can be reached easily in a day from Budapest, and coach tours are the best way to enjoy a jaunt outside the city. Two of the most spectacular and interesting are Lake Velence, southwest of Budapest, and Lake Balaton (► 84). Both are a mecca for wildlife, especially birds. Common are the heron and egret, also the white stork – one of Europe's most familiar birds. The lakes are popular with visitors, but their size affords plenty of quiet spots for those just wanting solitude and peace.

Budapest's Famous

Statue of Liszt, Hungary's famous composer

Hungary's history stands shoulder-to-shoulder with heroes and famous people – not surprising, since its evolution to an independent nation state has been nothing less than tempestuous. Most, if not all, of Hungary's famous (sometimes infamous) people have, in one way or another, been associated with, or inspired by, Hungary's turbulent past. One outstanding character, ironically not a Hungarian, was Raoul Wallenberg, a Swedish attaché during World War II, who helped countless Jews avoid the concentration camps. Two statues in his honour stand in Budapest.

Musicians

Two composers of international renown are Franz Liszt (1811–86) and Béla Bartók (1881–1945). Liszt liked to think of himself as part gypsy, a musical identity beautifully borne out in perhaps his most famous work, the 'Hungarian Rhapsodies'. Similarly, Bartók drew on the gypsy tradition of music, a tradition still very much alive in Hungary today.

More Magyars
In the world of film, the arts, the sciences and music, Hungarians have made a huge contribution. The legendary Alexander Korda, one of the founders of the British film industry, was Hungarian. So also were the international film stars Tony Curtis and Zsa Zsa Gabor. Liszt and Bartók need no introduction, nor perhaps Egon Ronay, the British guru of gastronomy. The humble ballpoint pen, the biro, takes its name from an Hungarian inventor – Biró. A name never forgotten in the history of warfare is Edward Teller, one of the fathers of the H-bomb. And those lucky enough to be awarded the prestigious Pulitzer prize should thank its Hungarian founder, Joseph Pulitzer.

Literature

Historically, the most heroic poetic voice belongs to Sándor Petöfi (1823–49) whose work 'National Song' was the inspiration for those who, like himself, fought and died in the 1848–49 War of Independence. Another poetic voice of considerable influence, especially among Hungarian youth, is Attilla József (1905–37), who vehemently attacked the harmful effects of progressive technology. Today, György Konrád and Péter Esterházy are considered leading luminaries in Hungarian literature.

Politics

Admiral Miklós Horthy, who formed an uneasy alliance with Germany during World War II, is still remembered for his nationalist spirit and his yearning to regain Hungary's pride and lost lands after the tragic post-war settlement which virtually crippled the country. Also celebrated is János Kádár, Hungary's leader for 32 years, who successfully engineered Hungary away from Soviet totalitarianism to a more liberal form of socialism.

Top Ten

Above: *statue of rebel leader Ferenc Rakoczi*
Right: *colourful folk traditions*

1
Budavári Palota
(Buda Castle Palace)

 29C3

✉ 1250 Budapest, Pf. 31.

🕐 Open daily throughout the year; museums open 10–6

🍴 Fortuna (££)

🚌 Várbusz (bus to the Castle); tram: 18; funicular from Clark Ádám tér

♿ Difficult

✋ Museums cheap

❓ Guided tours up to 5 people ☎ 375 7533/631

ℹ Charge for camera and video camera use

By far the most grandiose building in Buda, yet ironically a palace whose royals have never been resident, only visiting guests.

No other building in Buda reflects so dramatically the turbulent history of the Castle district. Built in the second half of the 13th century by King Bela IV, after the invasion of the Mongуls, centuries of war, invasion and revolution have left little of its original architecture. Razed to the ground during World War II, it was later rebuilt in baroque style. A magnificent stairway leads to the entrance of the palace proper, where the steep east wall widens into the deep embrasure. Note the statue of Prince Eugene Savoy, leader of the military operations that forced the Turks finally to retreat.

The double middle wing of the palace, including the dome, houses the National Gallery, with its comprehensive collection of Hungarian painting and sculpture. To reach the other museums, walk through the narrow passage to the west side through a pretty garden square, where you will see the Mathias Well (depicted as a hunting scene), regarded as one of the most beautiful fountains in Budapest. The west wing houses the National Szecheny Library, with its collection of about 2 million books, and even more manuscripts.

At the south end of the courtyard is the entrance to the Budapest History Museum (▶ 33), where 2,000 years of the city's history can be seen, including the marvellous Renaissance stone collection which illustrates the former lavishness of the Palace of Matthias Corvinus.

Facing the museum's entrance is a glass door which takes you to the top of a steep flight of stairs. All that remains, or was possible to recover and reconstruct of the medieval royal castle and fortress, can be seen here. You may by this time feel inclined to spend a little time in the Husolo ('cooling off chamber') situated under the Great Hall, cellars where the king's courtiers came to get out of the hot sun.

Located in the grounds of the Royal Palace, and worth a closer look in themselves, are the Lions which guard the entrance of Oroszlános udvar, The Lion Courtyard, designed by János Fadrusz in 1904. With their grim looks, two of these stone animals seem intent on discouraging visitors. But those brave enough to enter the lions' den are then met by two more inside the gate, roaring angrily. The huge door in the gateway between the lions leads to an elevator which takes you down to the bottom of the wing overlooking Buda.

The Royal Palace, a treasure-trove of Hungarian art

2
Gellért-hegy
(Gellért Hill)

🕀 29C1

✉ Budapest I, XI

🕙 Open access

🍴 Citadella Restaurant (££)

🚌 27; tram 18, 19, 47, 49

♿ Limited

✋ Citadel: cheap

Rising to a height of 235m between Erzsébet (Elizabeth) and Szabadság (Liberty) bridges over the Danube, this is perhaps the best vantage point from which to see Budapest.

Named after Bishop Gellért (Gerard), who was given the unenviable task of converting the reluctant Magyars to Christianity, this hill provides a commanding view of Budapest, and overlooks the Elizabeth Bridge from which, according to legend, this poor soul was cast into the Danube by a bunch of stubborn heathens.

At the foot of the hill are the Rudas Fürdő (Rudas Baths) with their unmistakeable domed roof, and inside, their octagonal pool. Crowning the hill is the Citadella (▶ 34), a white-stoned fortress constructed to restore order in the aftermath of the 1848–9 War of Independence. Today, as a restaurant and dormitory-style hotel, it fortifies nothing more than the hungry and foot-weary.

The top of the hill is crowned by the Liberation, or Freedom Monument (▶ 47), a striking statue of a woman holding a palm branch aloft. It was raised by the Russians in 1947 and originally incorporated a Soviet soldier, complete with red flag – tactfully removed after the collapse of Communism.

Towards Liberty Bridge you can see the famous Gellért Hotel (▶ 36), once the headquarters of the so-called dictator Admiral Horthy. Now the houses and apartments of the well-heeled dominate this area.

Breathtaking views of Budapest from Gellért Hill

3
Halászbástya
(Fishermen's Bastion)

'We have just seen its replica at the confectionary exhibition, only slightly more sugary than the original. While the tourists are at the dinner table, Halászbástya is visited by teenage couples on their first kiss'.
(András Török, Budapest, A Critical Guide)

✛ 28B4

✉ Szentháromság tér, Budapest I

🕐 Open access

🍴 Restaurant Bierstube (££)

🚌 16, Várbusz

♿ None

✋ Cheap

A Disneyesque edifice, situated on the eastern edge of Castle Hill, opposite St Matthias Church, the bastion was built at the end of the 19th century to coincide with the city's millennial celebrations. Affectedly Gothic in style, it owes more, perhaps, to the precocious (even riotous) imagination of its architect, Frigyes Schulek, than to any serious architectural tradition. Its seven conical towers represent the tents of the seven Magyar tribes who once made their home here. It offers a great day out for the family, as well as spectacular views of the Danube and city. From here you can see the luxuriant, tree-canopied Margit-sziget (Margaret Island), and the bridges of the Danube misting in the distance.

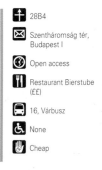

Round about the bastion, on Castle Hill, are numerous craft stalls and gift shops, though you might find their prices as inflated as the Bastion's architectural style.

Near by is the Magyar Nemzeti Galéria (Hungarian National Gallery ➤ 41) comprising four floors festooned with magnificent Hungarian cultural artifacts, including altarpieces, wood panels, paintings dating from the 13th to the 16th century, as well as works by modern and contemporary artists. A truly edifying contrast to the architectural absurdity of the Bastion.

Fishermen's Bastion is a beguiling architectural fantasy

A subtle contrast to both is Kereskedelmi és Vendéglátóipari Múzeum (Museum of Commerce and Catering ➤ 40), a museum devoted, perhaps oddly, to confectionary as well as to 19th- and 20th-century commerce. An intimate and cosy museum, and certainly more interesting than it sounds.

4
Magyar Állami Operaház
(Hungarian State
Opera House)

+ 52B4

✉ Andrássy út 22,
Budapest VI

☎ 353 0170; box office
311 9017

⊙ Guided tours: Mon–Sun
3 and 4. Box office:
Mon–Sun 11–7

🍴 Művész (£)

Ⓜ Opera

🚌 105, red 4

♿ None

✋ Guided tour: cheap.
Performance: regular
but not daily

Ranking among the most beautiful opera houses in Europe, you may find its opulence a distraction from the performance.

Commissioned by the Emperor Franz Joseph, the Opera's construction began in 1875 under the supervision of architect Miklós Ybl. Ybl apparently checked every cartload of stone. Italian-Renaissance in style, its interior is voluptuously marbled, gilded and decorated with frescoes by some of the finest painters of the time. It eventually opened in 1884 and attracted the biggest names in opera. Gustav Mahler was music director for a time, and after World War II Otto Klemperer took up the directorship. On the stone cornice of the terrace are statues of composers including Mozart, Verdi, Wagner and Beethoven; but niches by the main entrance are reserved for the great 19th-century Hungarian composers Erkel and Liszt. Above the vast auditorium, seating 1,289 people, hangs a three-tonne bronze chandelier decorated with a fine fresco by Károly Lotz showing Greek gods, with Apollo the god of music in the centre.

Despite its *fin-de-siècle* atmosphere, it is an entirely 'modern' building with all-metal hydraulic stage machinery, an iron curtain and even a sprinkler system. Closed in 1981 for extensive renovations, the Opera House was re-opened in all its former magnificence in 1984, exactly 100 years after the first performance here.

This building is a real treat, and should be one of the highlights of your itinerary. Tickets for performances are available from the box office, but beware: not all seats in the Opera House offer views of the stage.

The magnificent Opera House first opened its doors in 1884

5

Margit-sziget
(Margaret Island)

Adrift in the Danube, this idyllic island is the perfect escape from the hurly-burly of the city.

Citizens of Pest will claim, quite justifiably, that Margaret Island in the Danube is one of Europe's first parks. While not large by city park standards – it can be strolled through in about two hours – it's worth allowing plenty of time for leisurely exploration. It was originally three islands, and the Romans built the first bridge to connect them with the Buda shore. The largest island was called Rabbit Island, reflecting its status as a royal hunting reserve. Its present name was given in honour of King Béla's daughter Margit, who retired to a nunnery there in 1252, aged nine. During the Turkish occupation it was home to a rather different group – a harem.

Credit must go to the Hapsburg gardeners who planted many of the 10,000 and more trees on the island, most of them plane trees. Here, but under an oak tree, poet János Arany (1817–82) composed 'Under the Oak Trees'.

There are various amenities on the island, including a swimming pool, open-air cinema and theatre, a game reserve, rose garden, a Japanese garden and a garden of statues. At the northern end stands the famous old Grand Hotel (now the Ramada Grand Hotel), where the terrace offers a pleasant place in which to sit and enjoy the relaxed, tranquil atmosphere.

Enjoy the green spaces of Margaret Island

 Arrowed from 29C5

✉ River Danube – between Árpád and Margaret bridges, Budapest X111

🕐 Open access

🍴 Ramada Grand (£££)

🚌 26; tram 4,6

 Free

❓ Access by car from Árpád Bridge and then only as far as the car park next to the Ramada Grand Hotel, otherwise cars prohibited on the island

6
Mátyás-templom
(Matthias Church)

 28B4

 Szentháromság tér 2, Budapest I

355 5657

7AM–7PM. Collection of Ecclesiastical Art: Daily 9:30–5. Closed 14 Jan–11 Feb

 Restaurant Bierstube (££)

16, Várbusz

 Cheap to church; Collection of Ecclesiatical Art

Some claim this as a masterpiece of European eclectisism, while others compare it to over-decorated stage scenery.

Originally the church of the German burghers, and dedicated to the Blessed Virgin in Buda, its popular name derives from the fact that the legendary Hungarian king Mátyás (Matthias Corvinus, 1458–90) held both his weddings here. Parts date from the 13th century, but the main body of the church was extensively rebuilt in the 19th century. The dazzling, but muted, interior – the result of extensive restoration work carried out by Frigyes Schulek between 1874 and 1896 – recalls many of the original medieval designs. Note the beautiful floral motifs and geometric patterns on the walls. The Turks turned it into a mosque, and later it was converted into a baroque church. Schulek's dream was to restore it to as much of its original condition as possible, though his boundless enthusiasm for the ornate is all too evident, especially in the spectacular 80m-high spire.

Enter the church through the Mary Portal where you can see a 14th-century relief depicting the death of the Virgin. In the Loreto Chapel, to the left of the Mary Portal, is a gothic triptych and a baroque black madonna dating from 1700. By the main altar hangs the original coat of arms of Matthias Corvinus ('The Raven'). Two chapels, one dedicated to St Imre (son of St Stephen, the first Christian king of Hungary); the other, the Trinity Chapel, housing the tombs of the 12th-century king, Béla III and his wife, Anne of Châtillon, are to be found near the main door. Do not miss the impressive collection of ecclesiastical art, which is displayed in the two oratories.

Sumptuous stonework adorns Matthias Church on Castle Hill

7

Országház
(Parliament)

*Budapest's magnificent Parliament is a
vivid expression of Hungarian
national identity.*

A glorious Gothic pile bedecked with towers and
pinnacles, it was started in 1884, and finally completed in
1904. Today it remains a potent symbol of pride in the
then newly independent kingdom, and a testament of the
wealth of Hungary's industrial age.

The huge central dome is exactly 96m high – a
conscious and deliberate reference to the Magyar
conquest of Hungary in 896. It dominates a structure
which covers some 17,700sq m, encompassing ten
courtyards and hundreds of rooms. Directly beneath the
dome is a grand 16-sided hall, flanked to north and south
by individual chambers for the two houses of the
Hungarian parliament (now a single National Assembly).
Statues of prominent Hungarians occupy the central
hall (a bust of the Parliament's architect Imre
Steidl stands modestly off the main staircase), which
is still used for state occasions. Further statues of rulers
and military leaders adorn the outside of the
building, reinforcing the impression of a strong national
identity.

Not all commentators admire the building – one
Hungarian poet likened it, rather unkindly, to a
cross between a Gothic chapel and a Turkish bath –
but for many it is the outstanding example of
Gothic architecture on a grand scale to be seen in the
whole of Europe.

✝ 52A5

✉ Kossuth Lajos tér,
Budapest V

☎ Tours: 268 4437

🌐 Guided tours (in
English): Wed–Sun
10AM (when Parliament
is in session); Mon–Fri
10AM, 2PM, Sat 12:30PM,
Sun 10AM (during
recess)

🍴 Szalay (£)

Ⓜ Kossuth tér

🚌 15; tram 2; trolley bus
70, 78

♿ None

✋ Moderate

*View of the spired
Parliament building from
the Buda side*

8

Szent István Bazilika
(St Stephen's Basilica)

 52B3

 Szent István tér,
Budapest V

☎ 317 2859

🕐 Apr–Sep, daily 9–5;
Oct–Mar daily 10–4

🍴 Café Kör (£)

Ⓜ Arany János utca

 None

✋ Free

*The great dome of
St Stephen's stands
96m high*

*The vicissitudes of its construction might well have
tested even the patience of God Himself, for this
basilica took 55 years to build.*

This huge edifice, the largest church in the city, accommo-
dates 8,500 people. Construction started in 1851 and
wasn't completed until 1906, which gave rise to the local
joke 'I'll settle up when the basilica is finished'. The ground
plan of the basilica represents the shape of a Greek cross,
and is divided into nine barrel-vaulted parts, with a cupola
in the middle. No expense was spared in material glorifi-
cation: 41kg of 24-carat gold were used for the gilding,
while 88 statues adorn the exterior, celebrating, on the
Danube side, the Hungarian rulers, and on the Kossuth
side, the princes of Transylvania and several famous
commanders. Above the ground floor windows are the
lavish coats of arms of kings and princes.

The interior of this vast structure is ornamented with
paintings, tapestries, sculptures, and frescoes of the first
Hungarian artists: Mór Thán, Bertalan Székely, Gyula
Benczúr, Károly Lotz, Alajos Stróbl, János Fadrusz, Pai
Pátzay and Beni Ferenczy. The Holy Right (Szent Jobb), the
mumified right hand of St Stephen, the patron saint of the
church, preserved in a richly ornamented glass case, is the
most revered relic of the Hungarian Catholic Church.

Under the church is a large cellar where many
important documents and valuable art treasures survived
World War II. The windows of the basilica overlook Bajcsy-
Zsilinszky út, where a group of radical 1960s students
daubed the names of Lenin, Mao and Che – former
Communist revolutionary leaders, all of whom considered
religion to be 'the opium of the people'. The fading graffiti
on the wall is still visible.

9

Szépművészeti Múzeum (Fine Arts Museum)

If any institution demonstrates Hungarians' value of high art, it is this museum, which must rank as one of the major galleries in Central Europe.

With a collection of some 120,000 exhibits, this museum holds one of the finest Spanish collections outside Spain. The designers, Albert Schickedanz and Fölöp Herzog, completed the construction of the museum in 1906, and it represents the last piece of eclectic architecture in Hungary. The museum is ideally located in Heroes' Square, which is the grandest of Budapest's many open areas.

The Old Masters Gallery of the museum is world famous, exhibiting works by Raphael, Breughel, Rembrandt, El Greco, Velázquez and Goya, along with many more of the greats. British painting is well represented by Hogarth, Reynolds and Gainsborough. Also strongly represented are the French Impressionists and Post-Impressionists, including works by Delacroix, Courbet, Millet, Gauguin, Renoir, Monet, Cézanne and Toulouse-Lautrec. Picasso, Chagall, Le Corbusier and Vasarely bring the French collection into the 20th century.

If you haven't had enough by this time, there's also the Ancient Egyptian art collection which includes painted wooden mummy cases, reliefs from the wall of a temple built during the 4th century BC and some fine statuary. If you're a real glutton for art be sure to take in the Greco-Roman collection, and also the superb ceramics dating from the 6th to the 1st century BC. There is an enormous amount to get through in this collection, so you may wish to browse through some parts and concentrate on others.

✚ 75A3

✉ Hösök tere, Budapest XIV

☎ 343 7401

🕐 1 Jan–14 Mar, Tue–Sun 10–4, 15 Mar–31 Dec, Tue–Sun 10–6. Closed Mon

🍴 Bağolyvàr (£)

Ⓜ Hösök tere

🚌 4, 20, 30; trolley bus 75, 79

♿ None

✋ Cheap

❓ Guided tours; charge for camera and video use

The Fine Arts Museum is an impressive treasure-house of paintings and statuary

10
Várhegy
(Castle Hill)

Set on a limestone outcrop overlooking the River Danube, this old residential quarter of Buda is a place of unrivalled charm.

Though dating from the Middle Ages and earlier, sadly little remains of this area's medieval past – the result of successive wars and occupation by foreign powers. Painstaking reconstruction since World War II, when it was virtually destroyed, has however restored this area of Buda to a semblance of its once elegant Austrian baroque past. The wall of the castle is, in general, well preserved and offers a fine walk and spectacular views. Situated near the wall, close to Holy Trinity Column, is the statue of András Hadik, 'the most hussar of hussars', and the commander of Buda Castle between 1710 and 1790. Close inspection of his horse's rear end reveals that its testicles are shiny yellow. Touched by generations of students, allegedly they bring good luck! Houses 18, 20 and 22 on Országház utca (street), built in the 14th and 15th centuries, show what the Castle District might originally have looked like in the Middle Ages, while on the corner of Országház ucta and Kapisztrán tér (square) stands Mary Magdalene Tower, once a 13th-century church, and the only one allowed to remain a Christian church during Turkish rule. You will be hard-pressed to avoid the famous Ruszwurm pastry shop on Szentháromság tér (Trinity Square), whose aromas have entreated noses since it opened in 1827.

The opulent gateway to the castle gardens

Museums abound in the area, offering a variety of interesting exhibitions: in the Kereskedelmi és Vendéglátóipari Múzeum (Museum of Commerce and Catering ➤ 40), for instance, you can see a 40cm-long Easter rabbit-shaped mould, and the entire furniture and equipment of a small confectioner's in Buda. The Buda Castle Palace (➤ 16) houses the Contemporary Art Museum Ludwig Collection (➤ 41), Budapest History Museum (➤ 33), the Modern History Museum, the National Széchenyi Library (➤ 45), as well as the National Gallery (➤ 41).

What To See

Above: ornamental cherubs above Gellért Baths
Right: Prince Eugene of Savoy outside the Royal Palace

Familiar figures of traditional folk art

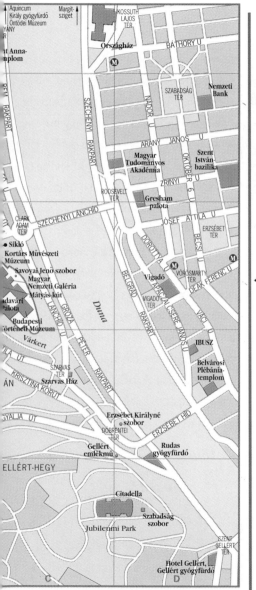

Below: *exponents of traditional horn music*
Bottom: *the evocative Freedom Monument*

Budapest

Not until as late as 1873, when the two districts of Buda and Pest were amalgamated, did the capital city of Budapest come into existence. But a lot of the Danube had flowed under its bridges by that time. The first major settlement here was Aquincum, a garrison town built by the Romans. Remains of their aqueduct and amphi-theatres can be seen just north of Óbuda. Buda itself, universally proclaimed as the centre of Renaissance learning during the 16th century, fell into terminal decline during the 150 years of Turkish occupation. The legacy of the Turks was their thermal baths, most of which still function today and are an unmissable treat. Pest, however, really didn't come into promi-nence until the 19th century when it became the focus of the city's cultural and commercial renewal under the Austrian Hapsburgs. Such was their passion for investment in the arts, shared by the Hungarians, that Budapest, almost overnight, became one of the major cultural cities in Europe, offering the visitor today an almost limitless choice of cultural venues.

> '*History has not spared the city, but could never destroy it*'

TOURIST OFFICE OF BUDAPEST

The City of Budapest

Buda

Though the vast width of the Danube separates Buda from Pest, its nine bridges and excellent public transport system provide easy access to both. You may want to start by visiting Buda first, a stroller's paradise, where you can wander at leisure through this 'museum of architecture,' sip a beer at one of its many bars or cafés, or indulge yourself culturally by visiting the numerous museums and galleries in the Castle District. The concentric design of the roads should ensure you never get lost.

Did you know ?

It is customary throughout Hungary to observe and celebrate the name day of relatives and friends. Such is the number of name days, every other day can be a celebration.

The spectacular Matthias Church, and the coat of arms of Freedom Bridge (opposite)

31

Parliament seen from above the Vienna Gate

 28A5
- Castle District, Budapest I
- Open access
- Pest Buda Restaurant (£)
- Bus 16, 78, Várbusz
- Free
- Cars are not allowed to enter the Castle District

What to See in Buda

BÉCSI KAPU (VIENNA GATE) ⭐⭐

The Gate is where all four streets that run the length of Castle Hill converge, and in the Middle Ages this was the place of the 'Saturday Market' for non-Jewish merchant traders. The story goes that any loud-mouthed Hungarian child would be scolded by being told his mouth was 'as big as the Vienna Gate'.

Climb to the top of the Gate and enjoy the panorama of Buda and the view of the Lutheran church in the square. There are also fine views of the unmistakable Parliament building across the Danube. Next to the bastion wall, to the right of the gate, is a small grove, the 'Europe Grove'. It gets its name from the time when the mayors of cities all over Europe brought and planted rare trees here, for example, Turkish hazel, Japanese cherry and cherry laurel.

> ### *Did you know ?*
> *Before the collapse of Communism and the fall of the Berlin Wall, Hungary was the only country where East and West Germans were permitted to meet.*

BUDAI LABIRINTUS (CASTLE LABYRINTH) ✪✪✪

The entrance on Uri utca 9 leads to an underground labyrinth of passageways stretching for about 10km beneath Castle Hill. These fascinating caves were joined together by the Turks for military purposes and today a section of about 1.5km can be explored. A waxwork exhibition (not to everyone's taste) is located here – a memorial of Hungarian history which is both light-hearted and serious. The exhibition recounts Hungary's mythological beginnings and finishes in the flourishing Renaissance Court of King Matthias. Oddly, nothing of Hungary's more recent and inglorious times is included. Only a street sign on the wall recalls the bitter years of World War II when thousands of people took refuge here from the siege. Not recommended for those who suffer from claustrophobia.

✚ 28B4
✉ Uri utca 9, Budapest I
🕐 Daily 10–6, closed Mon
🍴 Catacombs (££)
🚌 16, Várbusz
♿ Moderate
ℹ Guided tours only

BUDAPESTI TÖRTÉNETI MÚZEUM ✪✪✪
(BUDAPEST HISTORY MUSEUM)

Occupying the southern end of the Buda Castle Palace, Wing E, this excellent exhibition provides a historical record of Budapest's last 2,000 years. In the basement front hall of the History Museum there's a plaster model of Castle Hill, and a detailed drawing in black and white of the Gothic Buda Castle Palace as it probably used to be. Its largest hall was 70m by 17m, where even horseback tournaments took place! The museum is divided into two sections. On the lower level (a bewildering maze of passageways, cellars and vaulted halls) can be seen the remains of the medieval palace, together with sculptures, pots and pans, and weapons. Above is the principal exhibition, comprehensively documenting Budapest's long history, and containing photographs, prints and posters and, perhaps surprisingly, surviving artefacts from the Turkish occupation.

✚ 29C3
✉ Buda Castle Palace (Wing E), Budapest I
☎ 355 8849
🕐 Mar to mid-May and mid-Sep to Oct, Mon, Wed–Sun 10–6; mid-May to mid-Sep, daily 10–6
🍴 Café Pierrot (£)
🚌 Bus: 5, 16, Várbusz; tram: 18; funicular
♿ None
💰 Cheap

BUDAVÁRI PALOTA (BUDA CASTLE PALACE) (► 16, TOP TEN)

A battle-scarred exhibit at the fascinating History Museum

+ 29D1
☒ Budapest I and XI
⫟ Citadel (££)
⏱ Open access
🚌 Bus: 27; tram: 18, 19, 47, 49
♿ None
❓ A magnificent fireworks display takes place on Géllert Hill on 20 Aug

---

+ 29D2
☒ Döbrentei tér, Budapest I
🚋 Tram 18

A fine honour to Hungary's beloved Queen Elizabeth

CITADELLA (CITADEL) ⭐⭐

This grim, formidable stronghold on top of Gellért-hegy (Gellért Hill) was built after the Revolution of 1848–9, its principal miltary purpose to control Castle Hill. Parts of it were symbolically demolished in 1894. In the past it had several functions, as a prison camp, temporary accommodation for the homeless, the site of an anti-aircraft battery, and latterly a tourist attraction. Since it's a unique viewing point to look down on the city (telescope hire available), it is worth the walk. The 14m-tall statue of a woman holding a palm leaf is the Statue of Liberty and commemorates liberation from Fascist occupation.

ERZSÉBET KIRÁLYNÉ SZOBOR ⭐
(STATUE OF QUEEN ELIZABETH)

The statue, commemorating the assassination of Queen Elizabeth, wife of Franz Joseph, was originally situated on the Pest side of the Danube. Apparently the nation went into deep mourning on the news of her death, since she was beloved by all Hungarians and could speak Magyar. Before the last war another statue inhabited the site, that of an ultra-right wing politician who encouraged Hungary to ally with the Germans. Communist resistance fighters blew it up. A tablet in the ground near Elizabeth's statue commemorates this event.

GELLÉRT EMLÉKMŰ (GELLÉRT MONUMENT) ✪✪

Facing the Buda end of Elizabeth Bridge, the monument was erected in 1904, and is one of the ten royal statues donated to the capital by Emperor Franz Joseph. Impressive though it is – especially at night when floodlit – its story is more interesting. It was from the top of Gellért Hill, where the monument stands, that St Gellért (Gerard), the Bishop of Csanád, was pushed by pagan Hungarians he had come to convert to Christianity. After this ignominious fall, legend tells that he was nailed up in a barrel and thrown unceremoniously into the Danube.

GELLÉRT-HEGY (GELLÉRT HILL) (➤ 18, TOP TEN)

HALÁSZBÁSTYA
(FISHERMAN'S BASTION) (➤ 19, TOP TEN)

✚ 29D2
✉ Gellért-hegy, Budapest
🕐 Open access
🍴 Duna Restaurant, Hotel Gellért (££)
🚌 Bus: 27; tram: 18, 19, 47, 49
♿ None
🎟 Free

The impressive but forlorn statue of St Gellért

35

<

WHAT TO SEE

HILTON HOTEL ⭐⭐

Occupying a prime site in the Castle District on Hess András tér, the hotel was completed in 1976. Unobtrusive as it is, and blending well with the surrounding buildings, the president of the Hilton chain called this hotel the 'pearl in the whole string'. The old Jesuit cloister built in the late-rococo style forms one side of the hotel, and the Gothic remains of a Dominican church are enclosed by the hotel in such a way that it can be visited. Sumptuous, but understated, the hotel's interior has been carefully designed to capture the mood and atmosphere of the old town. Non-residents are welcome.

28B4
✉ Hess András tér 1–3, Budapest I
☎ 488 6600
🍴 Dominican Restaurant (££)
🚌 Bus: 5, 16, 78, Várbusz; tram: 18; Funicular
♿ Good

The sumptuous interior of the Hilton Hotel

HOTEL GELLÉRT ÉS GELLÉRT GYÓGYFÜRDŐ ⭐⭐⭐
(GELLÉRT HOTEL AND GELLÉRT THERMAL BATHS)

Described by a local illustrator as a 'huge white gem', the Danubius Gellért Hotel (to give it its full name) is one of the most prestigious in Budapest. The hotel, together with its thermal baths, was built as part of a major civic policy to make Budapest into a city of baths. If not taking a dip, then have a look at the mosaic floor and glass ceiling. From the back of the hall you can see into the roofed part of the swimming pool. Also see the outdoor pool, which was recently enlarged, its polished post-modern lines contrasting with the bulky art-nouveau building which was completed in 1918. The outdoor pool stretches to the other side of Kemenes utca and is connected to the main area by a subway. But if you're not feeling energetic, then relax with an ice-cream or a beer on the terrace.

29D1
✉ Hotel: Szent Gellért tér 1, Budapest XI. Baths: Kelenhegyi út 2–4, Budapest XI
☎ Hotel: 385 2200. Baths: 366 6166
🍴 Duna Restaurant (££)
🚌 Bus: 7, 7a, 86; tram: 18, 19, 47, 49
♿ Few
💧 Hotel: free; Baths: free if a resident of the hotel, otherwise moderate

Opposite: *thermal bathing in architectural splendour*

In the Know

If you have only a short time to visit Budapest, or would like to get a real flavour of the city, here are some ideas:

10

Ways to Be a Local

- **Learn a few words** of Hungarian and wait for an appreciative response.
- **Eat at locals' restaurants**, even if they seem a bit scruffy, and tip generously.
- **Drive assertively but politely**, if you dare.
- **Be inquisitive** about Hungary's history and culture.
- **Be polite**: local manners are formal with much shaking of hands.
- **Don't be brash** and ostentatious, especially with money.
- **Drink Hungarian brandy** without exploding!
- **Show an appreciation** of Hungarian cuisine and wine.
- **Don't stare** at Hungarians; they don't like it.
- **Remember that Budapest**, like the rest of Hungary, is part of Central Europe – not Eastern Europe.

Relax by the Danube, where pleasure boats ply its waters

10

Good Places to Have Lunch

Astoria Empire (££) ✉
Kossuth Lajos utca 19–21, Budapest V ☎ 317 3411. Fine food in elegant surroundings in the restaurant of the impressive Astoria Hotel (➤ 95).

Belcanto (££) ✉
Dalszinház utca 8, Budapest VI ☎ 269 3101. By the Opera House, serves good international cuisine. Waiters sing well-known operas.

Corvinus Restaurant (££) ✉ Erzsébet tér 7–8, Budapest V ☎ 429 3777. Innovative cuisine and cosy atmosphere (➤ 95).

Cyrano (££) Kristóf tér, 7–8, Budapest V ☎ 266 3096. Finely designed interior which served as a film location for *Cyrano de Bergerac*. Good wine selection (➤ 95).

Dominican (££) ✉ Hilton Hotel, Hess András tér 1–3, Budapest I ☎ 488 6757. Reasonably priced hotel restaurant, good stopping place if you are in the Castle District (➤ 92).

Fatál (££) ✉ Váci utca 67, Budapest V ☎ 266 2607. Homestyle Hungarian cooking – cash only (➤ 96).

Gundel (£££) ✉ Állatkerti körút 2 (or út 2), Budapest XIV ☎ 321 3550. Hungary's most famous restaurant. Dine in *fin-de-siècle* splendour. On the edge of City Park (➤ 96).

Kisbuda Gyöngye (££) ✉ Kenyeres utca (or út) 34, Budapest III ☎ 368 6402. *Fin-de-siécle* salon serving Hungarian specialities (➤ 93).

Múzeum Kávéház (££) ✉ Múzeum körút 12, Budapest VIII ☎ 338 422. High standard of decor and cusine (➤ 97).

Treat yourself to a night out at the opera

Robinson (££) ✉ Városliget Lake, Budapest XIV ☎ 422 0222. You pay for the romantic lakeside location by Heroes' Square (➤ 97).

10
Top Activities

A boat trip on the Danube (☎ 353 0558)
A coach city tour with stops (☎ 342 2335)
See Budapest from the sky in a hot-air balloon (☎ 322 0015)
A walk around Castle Hill – set a day aside
Museums: visit some of the many splendid museums
A romantic evening such as a 'Hungarian Evening on Margaret Island' – Taverna Tourist Service (☎ 318-1818)
'Take the waters' at one of the many thermal baths
A night at the opera is a real treat
Laze by the river all afternoon after a good picnic lunch
Walk in the Buda Hills

5
Best Views

- **Várhegy** (Castle Hill, ➤ 26) and Gellért-hegy (Gellért Hill, ➤ 18)
- **The lookout tower** on János-hegy (János Hill)
- **The lookout tower** on Josef-hegy (Josef Hill)
- **The dome** of Szent István Bazilika (St Stephen's Basilica, ➤ 24)
- **The terrace** of the Bellevue Restaurant, Mariott Hotel

10
Best for Children

- **Állat-és Növénykert** (Municipal Zoological and Botanical Gardens, ➤ 108)
- **Fővárosi Nagycirkusz** (Municipal Circus, ➤ 108)
- **Gyermek Vasút** (Children's Railway, ➤ 109)
- **Libegő** (Chairlift, ➤ 109)
- **Magic City** (➤ 108)
- **Palace of Wonders: Interactive Scientific Playhouse** (➤ 109)
- **Planetárium** (➤ 109)
- **Sikló** (Funicular, ➤ 47)
- **Urania Observatory** (➤ 109)
- **Vidámpark** (Amusement Park, ➤ 108)

39

28B4
Fortuna utca 4, Budapest I
375 6249
Wed–Fri 10–5, Sat, Sun 10–6
Restaurants near by (££)
Bus: 5, 16, 78, Várbusz; tram: 1
Limited
Cheap

Arrowed from 29C5
Fő utca 82–4, Budapest II
202 3688
Café (£)
Men: Mon, Wed, Fri 9AM–8PM; Women: Tue, Thu, Sat 6:30AM–6PM (12 Sat)
Batthyány tér
Bus: 60, 86
Few
Cheap

KERESKEDELMI ÉS VENDÉGLÁTÓIPARI MÚZEUM ✪✪ (MUSEUM OF COMMERCE AND CATERING)

This intimate and homely museum was built on the foundations of three medieval houses in the early 1700s. On the left are three rooms used by the Museum of Catering Trades, where an entire 19th-century cake shop has been relocated, with pastry kitchen and all the old equipment. Unlike many museums, the staff here are most helpful and personable. It's only a pity they can't re-create that gorgeous smell of freshly baked bread.

KIRÁLY GYÓGYFÜRDŐ ✪✪✪ (KIRÁLY THERMAL BATHS)

Considered to be one of the most famous thermal baths in Hungary, this is the place to come for a course of complete revitalisation. Besides the thermal pool, there are tub baths, salt baths and massage and sauna services. Built on a former Roman military road, the baths were constructed by the Turkish Pasha of Buda, Arslan, in the 16th century. It was then bought by the König family, from which the name Király stems. The building's Turkish decor and styling, especially the cupolas, make it an architectural masterpiece.

The architecturally splendid Király thermal baths

KORTÁRS MŰVÉSZETI MÚZEUM (CONTEMPORARY ART MUSEUM – LUDWIG COLLECTION) ✪✪

Based in Wing A of the Buda Castle Palace, the museum has had a chequered history and is certainly worth a visit. Originally called the Museum of the Working Class Movement, by the time the totalitarian regime began to crumble, the name was considered rather gauche. It received its new name and a billionaire patron in the late 1980s. Its collection is very contemporary, with only very recent works exhibited. Some claim it to be a very strong collection – witty, entertaining, even funny. Much the same could be said of the interior of the building with its red marble walls and oversize stairs.

🞢 28C3
✉ Buda Castle Palace (Wing A), Budapest I
☎ 375 9175
🕐 Tue–Sun 10–6
🍴 Restaurants and cafés near by (££)
🚌 Bus: 5, 16, 78, Várbusz; trolley bus: 18
♿ None
💲 Cheap

Left: *contemporary art in the Ludwig Collection*
Above: *an older treasure in the National Gallery*

MAGYAR NEMZETI GALÉRIA (HUNGARIAN NATIONAL GALLERY) ✪✪✪

Occupying Wings B, C and D of the Buda Castle Palace, the exhibition of Hungarian painting from the 19th century is perhaps the most evocative of all, the Hungarian word, *honfibu* (patriotic sorrow) best describing it. Hungarian painting found its natural style in the Romantic era, a style of profound sentiment. Of the Hungarian artists exhibited here, Kosztka Tivadar Csontváry's work is unparalleled. When Picasso saw his paintings, so the story goes, he asked to be left alone in the room with the doors locked. Most of Csontváry's paintings can be seen in a museum in the city of Pécs, about 200km outside Budapest (▶ 88).

🞢 29C3
✉ Buda Castle Palace (Wings B, C and D), Budapest I
☎ 375 7533, 375 7631
🕐 Tue–Sun 10–6
🍴 Restaurants and cafés near by (££)
🚌 Bus: 5, 16, 78, Várbusz; tram: 18; Funicular
♿ None
💲 Cheap
❓ Guided tours

41

MARGIT-SZIGET (MARGARET ISLAND) (► 21, TOP TEN)

MÁRIA MAGDOLNA-TORONY ⭐⭐
(MARY MAGDALENE TOWER)

28A4
✉ Kapisztrán tér 6,
Budapest I
🕐 Daily, 10–6
🍴 Restaurants and cafés
near by (£)
🚌 Bus: 16, Várbusz
♿ None

Situated on the corner of Országház utca and Kapisztrán tér, this 13th-century church was built for Hungarian worshippers on the border with a German parish. During Turkish rule special dispensation was given to the church to allow it to remain Christian, while all other churches were converted to mosques. Unfortunately the chancel and nave were destroyed during World War II, and have not been rebuilt, except for one stone window as a memento. Worthy of note are the serried ranks of 24 bells. A modern addition, their chime is like tumbling icicles.

MÁTYÁS-KÚT (MATTHIAS WELL) ⭐

29C3
✉ Castle Hill, Budapest I
🕐 Open access
🍴 Restaurants and cafés
near by (££)
🚌 Bus: 5, 16, 78, Várbusz;
tram: 18; funicular

Standing in the grounds of the Buda Castle Palace, the well has a bronze statue of King Matthias as a huntsman, in the company of his shield bearer and his Italian chronicler. The statue includes the figure of Szep Ilonka (Helen the Fair), a beautiful girl of low birth who fell in love with the King while he was hunting – a case of unrequited love. This most impressive statue is well worth seeking out.

MÁTYÁS-TEMPLOM (MATTHIAS CHURCH)
(► 22, TOP TEN)

Opposite: *all that remains of the humble church of Mary Magdalehe*

The statue of King Matthias is considered the finest in Hungary

🕇 Arrowed from 29C5
✉ Bem József utca 20,
  Budapest II
☎ 202 5327
🕘 Daily 9–5
🍴 Kacsa (££)
Ⓜ Batthyány tér
🚌 Bus 11, 60, 86; tram 4,6
♿ Possible
✋ Cheap

🕇 28B4
✉ Országház utca 18, 20,
  22, Budapest I
🍴 Miro (£)
🚌 5, 16, 78; Várbusz; tram:
  18; funicular

*One of the few remaining
dwellings originating
from medieval times*

ÖNTÖDEI MÚZEUM (FOUNDRY MUSEUM)　✪✪

This museum goes to prove how enterprising the
Hungarians are in turning an otherwise uninspiring industrial process into something of general interest. Built on
the site of the old Ganz ironworks, which produced the
world's first electric railway engine, the museum contains
a reconstructed foundry and workshop, also an interesting
collection of products once manufactured here. A quirky
idea, perhaps, but it provides an interesting insight into the
kind of heavy industry which characterised Hungary's
economy, particularly during the Communist era.

ORSZÁGHÁZ UTCA 18, 20, 22　✪✪

Built in the 14th and 15th centuries, these three houses
show what the Castle District may have looked like in the
Middle Ages. Italian craftsmen working on the Royal
Palace once lived here, lending their name to the street.
The initials inscribed on the gate of the middle house are
those of Johann Nicki, the butcher who had the house
rebuilt in 1771. The rear-view mirror on one of the
windows was to allow the person inside to check who
was at the front door.

ORSZÁGOS SZÉCHENYI KÖNYVTÁR (NATIONAL SZÉCHENYI LIBRARY) ✪✪

Yet another major site in the Buda Castle Palace, this library stocks over 2 million books, and even more manuscripts, musical scores and newspapers. Among these are the few remaining codices (maunscript volumes) from King Matthias's celebrated library. The codices are called Corvinas, and refer to the raven – the King's heraldic bird. The Main Reading Room, made up of several smaller rooms, is spacious but not especially elegant. Delightfully small carriages deliver and retrieve the books.

🕂 29C3
✉ Buda Castle (Wing F), Budapest I
☎ 224 3741
🕐 Tue–Sat 9–9, Mon 1–9
🍴 Restaurants and cafés near by (££)
🚌 Bus:5, 16, 78, Várbusz; tram: 18; funicular
♿ Limited
💰 Cheap

RÉGI BUDAI VÁROSHÁZA (OLD TOWN HALL) ✪✪

This imposingly quaint building, formerly the seat of the city's council, is now an Institute for Advanced Studies. The first session of the Council was held here in 1710, but its governing function came to an end in 1873 when Buda and Pest were united. The fine proportions of the Old Town Hall's windows and inner forked staircase suggest erstwhile political harmony. The statue (actually an Italian copy) on the corner of the building represents Pallas Athena, the guardian of towns. Reminiscent of some of the smaller Oxford colleges, this is a bustling place during term-time. Don't feel reticent about visiting it during this time, as the students and staff are most welcoming.

🕂 28B4
✉ 1, Szentháromság utca 2
🕐 Officially not open to the public, but visitors welcome
🍴 Alabárdos restaurant ££
🚌 5,16,78, Varbusz; tram 18
♿ Few

An illuminated manuscript dating from around 1485, displayed in the National Library

45

29C3

Front entrance, Buda
Castle Palace, Budapest I

Bus: 5, 16, 78, Várbusz;
tram: 18; funicular

*The graceful spans of
Freedom Bridge across
the Danube*

SAVOYAI JENŐ SZOBOR
(STATUE OF EUGENE OF SAVOY) ★

Opposite the entrance to the Buda Castle Palace on the
Danube side is the powerful and rousing equestrian statue
of the famous Prince Eugene of Savoy (1663–1736).
Born in Paris, following his father's death and his
mother's subsequent banishment from the French court
by Louis XIV, the Prince renounced the country of his birth
and joined the service of Emperor Leopold I in the fight
against the Turks. In a distinguished career he inflicted
heavy defeat on the Turks at Zenta, thus ending their
control in Hungary. However, unlike those of his
predecessors, this victory did not result in the plundering
of the country.

SIKLÓ (FUNICULAR) ✪✪

This is not just worth seeing, but is also fun to ride. Opened to the public in 1870, like the rest of the Castle District it suffered irreparable damage during World War II, and was rebuilt in 1986. Originally the railway was steam powered and adroitly used the passengers and car going downwards to pull the passengers in the other car upwards. You can enjoy a wonderful view of the Pest area from the funicular. The ride from the Buda end of the Chain Bridge up to Castle Hill takes two minutes. The car also carries prams and wheelchairs. Buy your tickets there.

Buda's funicular, part of the city's excellent public transport system

🕂 29C3
✉ Clark Ádám tér (lower terminus), Szent György tér (upper terminus), Budapest I
🕐 7:30AM–10PM. Closed every other Mon
🚌 Bus: 4, 16; tram: 19
♿ Good
👋 Cheap

SZABADSÁG HÍD (FREEDOM BRIDGE) ✪

This masterpiece of aesthetic engineering was opened in 1896 as part of the millenium celebrations, when Emperor Franz Joseph himself hammered in the final rivet. 'When designing the bridge,' said its architect, Virgil Nagy, 'I had to obey the requirements of beauty, simplicity and economy.' On top of each pillar, surmounting a golden ball, is a Turul bird, Hungary's mythical bird. .

🕂 52B1
✉ Szent Gellért tér, Budapest XI to Fővám tér, Budapest I
🍴 Duna Restaurant, Hotel Gellért (££)
🚌 Tram: 47, 49, 18, 19; bus: 86, 7, 7a

SZABADSÁG SZOBOR (LIBERATION MONUMENT) ✪

Situated by the Citadella as a sombre reminder of Budapest's more recent turbulent past, the Liberation (or Freedom) Monument commemorates the Soviet-led liberation of the city from the Germans in 1945. Originally intended to honour the dictator Admiral Horthy's son (a young pilot who died in a crash believed to have been engineered by the Germans), the monument was adapted by the Communists to reflect a new era, with the addition of a soldier figure and the inscription: 'To the liberating Soviet heroes from a grateful Hungarian people.' However, few Hungarians who lived through that time shared the sentiment, and the monument has been adapted again.

🕂 29D1
✉ Citadella, Budapest I
☎ 175 6451
🕐 Open access
🍴 Aranyszarvas (£)
🚌 Bus: 16, 78, Várbusz; Funicular
👋 Free

🕂 29C2
✉ Szarvas tér, Budapest I
☎ 375 6451
🕐 10AM–midnight
🍴 Aranyszarvas (£)
🚌 Bus: 16, 78
♿ None
🎫 Free

🕂 29C3
✉ Clark Ádám tér, Budapest
I to Roosevelt tér,
Budapest V
🍴 La Fontaine (££)
🚌 Bus: red 4, 16; tram: 2,
19

*The mighty Széchenyi
Chain Bridge was rebuilt
after World War II*

SZARVAS-HÁZ (DEER HOUSE) ⭐⭐

This triangular-shaped café was built at the beginning of
the 18th century in late-rococo style. Famous for its game
dishes, it's now the Aranyszarvas Restaurant. The Deer
House was once part of the Tában, a popular place of
entertainment on the northern slope of Gellért Hill. Many
of the houses here, apart from the Deer House, were
demolished for public health reasons. All the more reason
to eat at the Deer House, which is scrupulously clean.

SZÉCHENYI LÁNCHÍD ⭐⭐
(SZÉCHENYI CHAIN BRIDGE)

A symbol of Budapest and the first bridge over the
Danube, the crossing was built between 1839 and 1849
on the initiative of Count István Széchenyi. It was
designed by an Englishman, William Tierney Clark, and
built by his namesake Adam Clark.

During the country's War of Independence, the first
carriage to cross the bridge (at a time when it was still
under construction) carried the Hungarian crown from
Buda, which was then under siege, to Debrecen. Later,
the Austrian troops decided to blow the bridge up – but
the ever-resourceful Adam Clark frustrated their attempt
by flooding the explosive-packed chain chambers with
water. However, the Széchenyi Chain Bridge was
eventually blown up during World War II. It re-opened
again on 20 November 1949, exactly 100 years after its
original inauguration.

SZENTHÁROMSÁG SZOBOR
(HOLY TRINITY COLUMN)

Situated in the middle of Szentháromság tér near Matthias Church, the highest point on Castle Hill, the 14m-tall monument was erected between 1710 and 1713 by the inhabitants of Buda. It was hoped it would fend off further plague epidemics that had sporadically ravaged the city.

28B4
Szentháromság tér, Budapest I
Restaurant Bierstube (££)
16, Várbusz

ÚRI UTCA 31 (GENTLEMANLY STREET 31)

This endearingly named street in the Castle District has the distinction of the only row of houses in the area to run in a north–south direction. The façades are later additions, but the courtyards, the ground floors, the gateways with their recessed benches, and the cellars, are authentically medieval, and well worth seeing. This is a place where you can literally step into the past – but do it in a gentlemanly way.

28B4
Úri utca, Budapest I
Miro (£)
Bus: 5, 16, 78, Várbusz; tram: 18; funicular

Step into medieval times in Úri utca

VÁRHEGY (CASTLE HILL) (▶ 26, TOP TEN)

VÁRSZÍNHÁZ (CASTLE THEATRE)

Completed in 1736, the building was originally the Church of the Order of Our Lady of Mount Carmel, but in 1784 Joseph II dissolved this order. The monastery then became a casino, and the church gave place to a theatre. The theatre had a wooden floor and could seat 1,200 people, and it was here that the first ever play in Hungarian was performed – previously all other performances had been in German. In 1924 a part of the gallery collapsed, postponing the next performance until 1978 when the new theatre, of marble and concrete (but seating only 264 people), was opened.

28B3
Színház utca 1–3, Budapest I
Daily
375 8011. Tickets for perfomances ☎ 322 7914, 267 3314, 212 5678
Restaurants and cafés near by, Rivalda (£££)
Bus: 5, 16, 78, Várbusz; tram: 18; funicular

Around Várhegy (Castle Hill)

Distance
Approx 1km

Time
1 hour, or 2 hours with stops

Start/end point
Disz tér
✚ 28B3
🚇 Castle line (signed 'V')
leave from Moszkva tér;
Várbusz; funicular from
Szent György tér

Lunch
Korona (£)
✉ Disz tér
☎ 175 6139

*Panoramic views from
Fishermen's Bastion
Inset: delightful detail
from Castle Hill buildings*

This walk round Castle Hill (➤ 26) gives a flavour of the old town of Buda.

From the cobbled Dísz tér (square) enter Tárnok utca.

At No 18 is the Patikamúzeum (Museum of Pharmacy), a former chemist's shop dating from 1745.

Walk towards Szentháromság tér. Pass to the right of St Matthias Church (➤ 22) into cobbled courtyards with the Halaszabastya (Fishermen's Bastion ➤ 19) in front of you.

Climb the towers of Fishermen's Bastion for spectacular views of the Danube and Pest.

Return via the north side of St Matthias Church with the Hilton Hotel (➤ 36) on your right. Back on the Szentháromság tér, turn right into Hess András tér, then bear left and walk down Fortuna utca.

Fortuna utca is perhaps the most picturesque street on Castle Hill. On the

left, the Museum of Commerce and Catering (➤ 40) is worth a visit.

Passing the high–class Café Pierrot, enter Bécsikapu tér, dominated by the Gothic edifice of the National Archives of Hungary. Walk up Petermann Bíró utca to the tower and ruins of medieval Mary Magdalene Church (➤ 42), then turn left towards Úri utca.

The pastel-green building on the right, with a police sign outside, houses the Telefónia Múzeum (Telephone Museum).

Return to Szentháromság tér. Turn left by the equestrian statue of Hadik András to Tóth Árpád sétány for distant views of the Buda Hills. Turn back, then right into Úri utca.

At No 9 is the entrance to the Catacombs (➤ 33). Many of the caves are believed to be between 500 and 700 years old and were used for military purposes by occupying Turks.

Walk down into Dísz tér, where the walk ends.

Floral abundance in Castle Hill's cobbled main square

51

Pleasure boats on the river

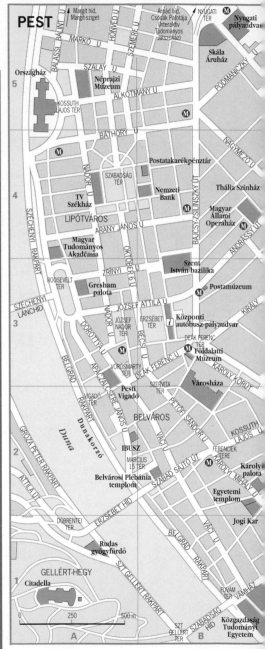

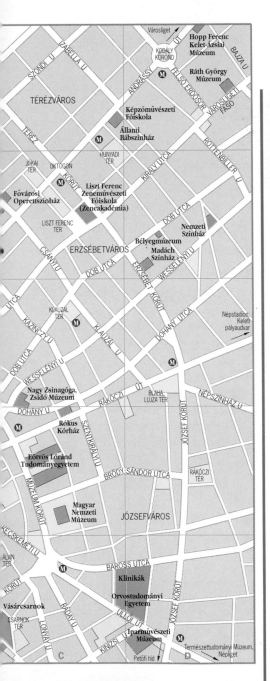

Városliget

Hopp Ferenc
Kelet-Ázsiai
Múzeum

KODÁLY
KÖROND

Ráth György
Múzeum

TÉRÉZVÁROS

Képzőművészeti
Főiskola

Állami
Bábszinház

HUNYADI
TÉR

Liszt Ferenc
Zeneművészeti
Főiskola
(Zeneakadémia)

OKTÓGON

JÓKAI
TÉR

Fővárosi
Operettszinház

LISZT FERENC
TÉR

Nemzeti
Színház

Bélyegmúzeum

ERZSÉBETVÁROS

Madách
Színház

DOB UTCA

Népstadion;
Keleti
pályaudvar

KLAUZÁL
TÉR

Nagy Zsinagóga,
Zsidó Múzeum

BLAHA
LUJZA TÉR

DOHÁNY U

Rókus
Kórház

Eötvös Lóránd
Tudományegyetem

RÁKÓCZI
TÉR

Magyar
Nemzeti
Múzeum

JÓZSEFVÁROS

BAROSS UTCA

ÁLVIN
TÉR

Klinikák

Orvostudományi
Egyetem

Vásárcsarnok

CSARNOK
TÉR

Iparművészeti
Múzeum

Természettudományi Múzeum,
Népliget

Petőfi hid

The Great Synagogue

Pest

For a taste of cosmopolitan city life, but with an unusual parochial flavour, Pest is a lavish collection of eclectic architectural styles – grandeur on an imperial scale. At street level, however, there is almost a village atmosphere, with an abundance of parks and gardens, small side-streets and inviting squares. The presence of the Danube, and the grid system of roads, some of which are pedestrianised, make finding your way around Pest very easy.

> *'The Danube separates the two cities, in other respects one. Buda is upon an eminence above the western, and Pest below upon the eastern bank. Pest is a very large and handsome city...'*

E D CLARKE
Travels in Various Countries
(1818)

Pest

It is said, perhaps unfairly, that when Pest wants to sleep it goes to Buda. The silt of the Danube piles up on the Buda side, while a swift current runs along the Pest bank. Pest is the commercial and entertainment hub of the city, and there's little sleep in this part of Budapest, which thrives on a tradition of music, good food, and a tireless night life. Pest has most of the best attractions, the restaurants, and the best hotels. It also has the best shopping. Laid out largely during the 19th century on the Paris pattern of boulevards and straight avenues, this is the only similarity to the French capital.

Ravaged by successive wars and conflicts, Pest has grown into a city of delightful eclectic uniqueness. Its tenacious sense of history and grandeur is apparent everywhere, especially in its architecture which ranges from shabby, almost derelict eloquence, to glorious sumptuousness. Buda might taunt Pest with its regal ambience, but Pest quite definitely is the more exciting.

The decorative and dizzying heights of the Parliament building dominate the Pest bank

The elegant Lukács coffee house on Andrássy Way

52B4
Andrássy út, Budapest V
Bombay Palace (£)
Oktogon

What to See in Pest

ANDRÁSSY ÚT (ANDRÁSSY WAY) ✪✪

Once the city's premier boulevard, it was named after the famous statesman, Andrássy. An architectural jumble of glorious opulence and fading splendour, at one time it was known as Stalin Avenue, and until recently was called by the equally uninspiring name Avenue of the People's Republic. It runs all the way from Deák tér to Városliget (City Park), is home to the State Opera House and the Academy of Fine Arts, as well as to almost a constant stream of traffic, which makes walking a bit hectic. There are some good shopping opportunities here, however.

Arrowed from 52A5
Árpád híd, Budapest III
Kéhli (££)
Bus: 26; tram: 1

ÁRPÁD HÍD (ARPHAD BRIDGE) ✪

Located north of Margaret Bridge, Arphad Bridge is the longest and most robust of the six bridges crossing the Danube in the vicinity of downtown Budapest and links the mainland with Margit-sziget (Margaret Island, ➤ 21). It's worth a walk across if only for the views it offers of the city and a sense of the immense breadth of the Danube, and Margaret Island is certainly worth a visit.

Budapest's VI District

The most illustrious part of the city in the late 19th century, the VI District is now a mixture of dilapidation and residual glamour.

Start outside the Opera House on Andrássy út.

Though often congested with traffic now, Andrássy út was once the Champs Elysées of Budapest, and its neo-Renaissance and baroque Opera House (► 20) is one of the finest in Europe.

Walk up towards the Oktogon and look out for the magnificent Művész Coffee House and the Párizsi Nagyáruház at No 29.

The latter was once an exclusive casino, and some of its former glory remains.

Past the grand villas is the Lukács Coffee House, newly restored to its former splendour, and the Kodaly körönd, sumptuously painted with delicate gold filigree. Before this is the Fine Arts Academy (► 25). After the Kodály körönd, go right along Bajza utca, past the old villas and diplomatic residences, to Városligeti fascor.

In the 19th-century, this grand boulevard with tree-lined pavements was used for horse-racing. Here at the boundary of the VI District you will see some wonderful art-nouveau villas and mansions.

Take a quiet break in the Epreskert, or Mulberry Garden, half-way along Bajza utca.

This is the Arts Academy sculpture garden with both baroque sculptures and modern works.

Meander back via Király utca and Hunyadi tér to the heart of the district. At the junction with Erszébet körút, turn right and head towards Liszt Ferenc tér on the left side.

Here is the Liszt Music Academy (► 77), its magnificent concert hall is a magnet for classical music lovers.

Turn left on to Andrássy út and return to the Opera House.

Distance
4–5km

Time
2–3 hours, or 5 hours with stops for refreshments and visits

Start/end point
Opera House
✚ 52B4
Ⓜ Opera

Lunch
Lukács (£)
✉ Andrássy út
☎ 132 1371

The awesome beauty of the Opera House

Above: Turkish prayer niche in the Inner City Parish Church (right)

52B2
Március 15 tér, Budapest V
317 9800
Daily
Mátyás Pince (£)
Ferenciek tér
Tram: 2
Good
Free

BELVÁROSI PLÉBÁNIA TEMPLOM (INNER CITY PARISH CHURCH)

✪✪✪

The church is situated close to Elizabeth Bridge on Március 15 tér in an area that was once the centre of the 4th-century Roman settlement of *Contra-Aquincum*. A small display of its remains can be seen there. Buttressed against the ugly flyover is this beautiful church, one of the oldest in the city. Dating from the 12th century, it was rebuilt in the 18th century after a devastating fire, hence the baroque façade and interior. At one time the Turks converted it into a mosque and you can still see a Muslim prayer niche or *mihrab* to the right of the high altar. If you can bear the flyover with all its traffic, delight in the beauty of this church and curse the city planners.

53C2
Dohány utca 2-8, Budapest VII
Great Synagogue: Mon–Fri 10–3, Sun 10–1
King's (£)
Astória
Bus: 7. 7/A, 78; tram: 47. 49; trolley bus: 74
None
Cheap

DOHÁNY UTCA (JEWISH DISTRICT)

✪✪

At the intersection of Dohány utca and Károly körút, at the heart of the old Jewish quarter, stands the Great Synagogue, the largest in Europe. Above the entrance the Hebrew line reads: 'Make me a sanctuary and I will dwell among them'. With its three naves and flat ceiling, the building holds 3,000 worshippers; 1,497 men on the ground floor and 1,472 women in the gallery. One of the buildings in the compound was the birthplace of Theodor Herzl, the father of the Zionist movement. Built in Moorish-Byzantine style, its two magnificent domes rise 43m in height. The Holocaust Memorial in the back garden is directly over the mass graves dug during the 1944–5 Hungarian fascist period, and on every leaf is the name of a martyr. The memorial is a grim reminder of the terrible suffering of the Hungarian Jews, and of their determination never to forget. The walls of some the buildings in the vicinity of the synagogue still bear the marks of bullets.

DUNAKORZÓ (THE PROMENADE) ✪✪

In the latter years of the 19th century much of neo-classical Pest was hidden by large hotels, some the finest and most fashionable in Europe – the Carlton, Ritz, Hungaria and the Bristol. This is where the rich and fashionable strolled during the summer months, a tradition that had survived from the time when Pest was a small town. It was especially beautiful in the evening with brightly lit cafés and jazz and gypsy music. Now with new hotels in the area, the promenade is coming to life again, though the Elizabeth Bridge end is rather seedy and a favourite haunt of prostitutes.

➕ 52A2
✉ Vigadó tér, Budapest V
🍽 Gerbeaud (££)
🚋 Tram: 2

Sombrely beautiful, the golden grounds of the Holocaust Memorial

🎯 52B3
✉ Deák tér, Budapest V
☎ 461 6500, 464 1103
🕐 Tue–Sun 10–6
🍴 Vista Café (£)
Ⓜ Deák tér
🚌 Bus: 9, 16, 105; tram: 47, 49
♿ None
✋ Cheap

FÖLDALATTI MÚZEUM (UNDERGROUND RAILWAY MUSEUM)

Hidden away in the metro station underpass on Deák tér, this tiny, exquisite museum occupies one of the original railway tunnels. Its exhibition includes a fascinating array of plans, models and carriages, and shows the development of the first underground system on the European mainland. The first line, completed in 1896, ran the entire length of Andrássy út, a distance of 3.5km.

The museum is definitely worth a visit if you're a keen train-spotter. Even if you're not exactly a train fanatic, it's something to keep in mind for a rainy day.

🎯 75A4
✉ Állatkerti kőrút 2, Budapest XIV
☎ 321 3550
🕐 Daily 12–4, 6:30–midnight
Ⓜ Hősök tér

GUNDEL ÉTTEREM (GUNDEL RESTAURANT) ⬤⬤

It's not unusual in Budapest to come across restaurants and cafés that are worth visiting not just for their food but also for their splendid architecture and décor. The unique thing about Gundel's is its first-rate collection of Hungarian masters on the walls; the menu helpfully supplies information about the paintings. Above the splendid dining room are the Elisabeth and Andrássy rooms, where some of the most elegant banquets in Budapest are held. As you would expect, the food is excellent and there's a seriously well-stocked wine cellar to complement your meal.

Did you know?

According to Hippocrates, the father of medical science, cures effected by water are one of the bases of medicine. Hungary's medicinal spa waters, drunk or bathed in, are said to cure up to 40 ailments, from kidney stones to receding gums.

HOPP FERENC KELET-ÁZSIAI MÚZEUM (FERENC HOPP MUSEUM OF EASTERN ASIATIC ART) ✪

This museum, one of two in the city devoted to major collections of Asian art, houses the treasures amassed by the Hungarian traveller Ferenc Hopp (1833–1919), who once lived here. Like so many of the smaller and quirkier museums in the city, it's a little gem, and if nothing else tells you as much about Ferenc Hopp himself – a compulsive, eccentric collector – as about the treasures of East Asia. Among the fascinating ancient exhibits are Buddhist works, and Indian art dating as far back as the 3rd century.

A wide-ranging collection of Chinese and Japanese exhibits are housed near by in the Ráth György Múzeum at 12 Városligeti fasor. Of the two collections, the former is arguably the more impressive.

✚ 53D5
✉ Andrássy út 103, Budapest V
☎ 322 8476
🕐 Tue–Sun 10–6 (5, Nov–Mar)
🍴 Lukács (£)
Ⓜ Bajza utca
🚌 Bus: red 4
♿ None
💷 Cheap

The epitome of gracious eating at Gundel's restaurant

Food & Drink

Ask anyone to name a Hungarian dish and the answer invariably will be goulash. They will also make the mistake of calling it a 'stew' when it is in fact a soup (a mistake I confess making). Perhaps because of decades of Communism, Central European cuisine has been associated with the sort of meal one would describe politely as filling, nutritious, yet unimaginative and bland – a misconception. Hungarian cooking can compete with the finest in Europe.

Characteristic Features of Hungarian Cooking

Traditional Hungarian 'peasant' cooking is based on the use of *rantas*, a rich roux of flour and pork lard. Bland and heavy, it requires lashings of paprika to spice it up. Paprika is still widely used and now thought of as a defining feature of Hungarian cooking. As the saying goes, 'a real Magyar can handle his strong paprika well'. Another characteristic is the use of sour cream, which adds a sharpness to the flavour. Soups and pasta also figure strongly, with the ever-present paprika either ready at hand on the table, or already in the dish. However, Hungarian cuisine prides itself on being rich, full of flavour, and substantial – which means you won't leave Hungary feeling hungry!

Paprika is the staple spice of much of Hungarian cooking

The Carnivore and the Vegetarian

Most, if not all, Hungarian menus are dominated by meat dishes. Favourite meats are chicken (their livers are a Hungarian speciality), pork, veal, venison, duck and beef. Sometimes you can discover, as with 'Tenderloin Steak Budapest Style', for instance, any number of different meats mixed together. In this case, the steak sits alongside smoked bacon, pork bones and goose livers. Hence Hungarian cuisine's reputation for richness. Fish is also well represented on Hungarian menus, especially pike, carp, perch and trout. Being a land-locked country, the scarcity of sea fish is not surprising, but if anyone can turn a pike or carp (fish generally frowned upon elsewhere) into a mouth-watering dish, it's the Hungarians.

Mouth-watering salamis, a favourite Hungarian food

Potent, but irresistible, Hungarian brandies are the real thing

Pike dumplings are delicious in a dill sauce, as is carp served with mushrooms in a sour cream sauce. But the vegetarian shouldn't entirely despair. Most restaurants, even those with hard-pressed staff, will be sympathetic to visitors' dietary preferences and palates.

Wines, Beers and Spirits

We are all familiar with Hungarian merlot and cabernet-sauvignon reds and whites, also with the legendary Egri Bikaver (Bull's Blood) which once rubbed corks on the lower shelves with popular *vins de table*. This wine is still very popular in Hungary, but for superior quality try Vesztzergombi Bikavér. Tokaji is what Louis XIV of France called 'the wine of kings, the king of wines'. Rumour has it that since so little of this exceptional white wine is produced from that region, you're bound to buy a fake bottle. This is not quite true. The best Hungarian beers are Kőbányai and Dreher, but you'll also find an abundance of familiar foreign brands.

Traditional Hungarian spirits are brandies called *pálinka*, and are available in various flavours. Be warned though: they are generally strong. Otherwise, all the usual spirits are available, for example whisky, vodka and gin. Those who prefer soft drinks can get anything from mineral water to cola.

Did you know?

With smoking under near universal attack, a group of Budapest entrepreneurs have instituted a unique 'Big Smoke' evening of cigars, including dinner, a cigar show and cigar memorabilia auction.
Tickets: Cigar Tower ✉ Kempinski Hotel Corvinus, Erzsébet tér 7–8 ☎ 266 1000

75A3

Budapest XIV

Open access

Lukács (£)

Hősök tere

Bus: 20, 30; red 4; trolley: 75, 79

Free

City Park, Museum of Fine Arts, Art Gallery

HŐSÖK TERE (HEROES' SQUARE) ●●●

At the top of Andrássy út, where it meets City Park, is Heroes' Square. The square forms a splendid unity of two architecturally diverse buildings – the Art Gallery and the Museum of Fine Arts – and a monument. The central feature of Heroes' Square is the Millennium Monument, a 36m-high column, on top of which stands Gabriel, the Guardian Angel. The colonnades on either side display statues of Hungarian kings and leading figures of the Hungarian independence wars. On the left wing are the allegoric bronze statues of War, Peace and Knowledge; on the right, statues representing War, Peace and Glory.

In the middle of the square, behind the column of Gabriel, is the picturesque group of statues of the conquering Magyars, with Árpád, the leading reigning prince, in the middle. The statue complex commemorates the 1,000th year of the Hungarian state. Dedicated to Hungary's heroes, its architectural design is particularly fitting, and leaves you with a deep sense of Hungarians' pride in their past.

Next to Heroes' Square is Procession Square, where processions and parades are held on public holidays. This was the site of a monolithic statue of Stalin which was torn down by Hungarian nationalists during the 1956 Uprising. Also here is the Tomb of the Unknown Soldier, where Soviet veterans still come to pay their respects.

Heroes' Square, where the great and good of Hungary are celebrated

The Museum of Applied Arts – an architectural gem of a building and a museum to rival the best in Europe

Earthenware jug, one of a rich collection of artefacts

IPARMŰVÉSZETI MÚZEUM (MUSEUM OF APPLIED ARTS) ✪✪

This fine museum was rebuilt in the 1950s after it was destroyed, like so many other treasured buildings, during World War II. The original building was in fact one of hundreds hastily built to mark the millennial celebrations of 1896. Designed by Ödön Lechner and Gyula Partos, the coloured ceramic-and-brick building blends an art-nouveau style with Hungarian folk motifs, which makes it a museum piece in itself. The aula is covered with a steel-framed glass ceiling. A pendulum once hung from here to show the rotation of the Earth as part of the exhibition on the history of measuring time, of which it eventually became a victim and was taken down.

If you can pull yourself away from its magnificent decor, there are fine collections of furniture, metalwork, textiles, woodwork, ceramics and glass to be seen, as well as examples of other handicrafts.

🚩 53D1
✉ Üllői út 33–7, Budapest IX
☎ 217 5222/171
🍴 McDonald's (£)
🕐 Tue–Sun 10–6
Ⓜ Ferenc körút
🚋 Tram: 4, 6
♿ Limited
✋ Cheap

KÖZLEKEDÉSI MÚZEUM (TRANSPORT MUSEUM) ✪✪

This delightful museum is ideal for children (and dads!). The exhibits include models of ships, cars, trains, motorbikes, aeroplanes and engines. It's the sort of place where you can become so absorbed, you forget the time. And there's a super restaurant on hand if you feel peckish, set in an old railway dining car. You can combine a visit to the museum with a pleasant stroll across the Városliget (City Park), one of the best parks in the city.

🚩 75C2
✉ Városligeti körút 11, Budapest XIV
☎ 343 0565
🕐 May–Sep, Tue–Fri 10–5, Sat, Sun 10–6; Oct–Apr, Tue–Fri 10–4, Sat, Sun 10–5
🍴 Railway car (£)
🚋 Tram: 1; trolley bus: 70, 72, 74
♿ Limited
✋ Cheap

MAGYAR ÁLLAMI OPERÁHÁZ (OPERA HOUSE) (► 20, TOP TEN)

 53C2
✉ Múzeum körút 14–16, Budapest VIII
☎ 338 2122
⏰ Tue–Sun 10–6 (5, mid-Oct to mid-Apr)
🍴 Astoria Empire (££)
Ⓜ Astoria, Kálvin tér
🚌 Bus: 9; tram: 47, 49
♿ Possible with help
▦ Cheap

The skeleton of an elephant is one of the exhibits in the Hungarian National Museum in Budapest

MAGYAR NEMZETI MÚZEUM (HUNGARIAN NATIONAL MUSEUM) ✪✪✪

The largest museum in the country, it was built between 1837 and 1847. Almost 8,000sq m in area, it has five independent departments: the Archaeological Collection, the Medieval Collection, the Modern Collection, the Numismatics Collection and the Historical Portrait Collection. Painstaking reconstruction gathered pace in 1944–5 in order to house the permanent History of Hungary exhibition. The exhibits include prehistoric tools and implements, artefacts from the period of Turkish occupation, and memorabilia from the 1848–9 War of Independence.

Some of its exhibits are a bit quirky, but the museum nevertheless offers a fascinating insight into Hungarians' prioritising of their history: for instance, in the long 19th-century room there is a full display of all the screws of a factory lovingly arranged on a large board. Another quirky exhibit in Room 1 is a brick, which once indicated the tomb of a monk in the 13th century, with the inscription: 'Why are you staring at me? The way I look now, it's your future fate. You'd rather say a Lord's Prayer.' The complete reconstruction of the museum is due to end in 2002.

The exhibition of Hungarian Royal Regalia, including the 11th-century Crown of St Stephen, has been transferred to the Parliament (► 23).

MAGYAR TUDOMÁNYOS AKADÉMIA (HUNGARIAN ACADEMY OF SCIENCES)

Though unfortunately not open to the public, this is an architecturally impressive building, not least because of the fine array of statues on the exterior façades. These statues, made to the plan of the building's architect, Friedrich Stuler, celebrate the great names of science and letters. Six statues of Galileo and Miklós Révai adorn the second floor, while Newton and Lomonosov, Descartes and Leibniz reside on other sections of the Academy building. Apparently the interior decor is sumptuous and very comfortable. Like most academic institutions, it has its rather arcane rules, one of them being that no more than 200 members are permitted to be under the age of 75.

The Academy shares Roosevelt tér with another fine building, Gresham Palace, a lavish art-nouveau structure which was once the headquarters of the Gresham Insurance Company.

52A4
Roosevelt tér, Budapest V
Lou Lou (££)
Tram: 2

An impressive façade adorns the Academy of Sciences

🚹 52A5
✉ Kossuth Lajos tér 12, Budapest V
☎ 312 4878
🕐 Tue–Sun 10–6 (4, Dec to Feb)
🍴 Café (£)
Ⓜ Kossuth tér
🚌 Bus: 15; tram: 2; trolley bus: 70, 78
♿ None
👍 Cheap

The imposing former palace houses a diverse collection of ethnographic artefacts

NÉPRAJZI MÚZEUM (MUSEUM OF ETHNOGRAPHY)   ✪✪✪

Strongly resembling the Reichstag in Berlin, but much more elegant, this neo-Renaissance palace was built to house the Supreme Court and the Chief Public Prosecutor's Office. Sculptures of legislators, magistrates and goddesses of justice adorn the façade of this formidably large and imposing building. Its grandiose entrance hall features a marble stairway, huge chandeliers, and on the ceiling a splendid fresco by Karoly Lotz..Again, this is worth visiting if only for its magnificent architecture and decor. Permanent exhibitions include diverse ethnological material from all over the world: from Inuit furs and kayaks to Melanesian masks. Highly interesting are the displays illustrating Hungarian peasants' way of life, culture and art.

> ### *Did you know ?*
>
> *Rather than destroy all the discredited Communist iconography – statues and posters of Marx and Lenin – after the collapse of Communism, the Hungarian authorities collected them together and placed them all in the grandly named Totalitarian Statue Theme Park in Balaton út, Budapest XXII.*

NYUGATI PÁLYAUDVAR (WESTERN RAILWAY STATION) ✪✪✪

Since trains depart from here for the north and east, the name is perhaps slightly misleading. Constructed by the Eiffel Company of Paris in the late 19th century, over the following 100 years this 25,000sq m hall started to deteriorate and plans were drawn up for a new building. Conservationists protested and eventually won the day, helping to preserve the principal iron structure. They gave in on the paintwork, however, which is now a light blue, apparently a post-modern favourite. Towards the end of the hall on the left is a large door, above which is carved: '*Viribus Units*' (With Unity Strength). The elegant glass screen of the station's main façade lets the trains merge with the city's traffic. About 20 years ago, one train did indeed leave the rails and merge literally with the traffic – it came to a halt at the tram stop! The giant restaurant room to the right of the main entrance is now a McDonald's, though, to their credit, they have retained the original elegance of the room.

✚ 52B5
✉ Nyugati tér, Budapest XIII
☎ Information: 349 8503
🕐 Open access
🍴 Nyugati (£)
Ⓜ Nyugati pályaudvar
♿ Few
✋ Free

The glass façade of the Western Railway Station offers travellers a window on the world

NÉPSTADION (PEOPLE'S STADIUM) ✪

This is Hungary's largest sports stadium, built by and for the people. The sturdy Stalinist statues outside are a reminder of the old regime. Opened in 1953, the stadium has a seating capacity of 76,000, but seldom attracts such numbers today – it is perhaps a testament of the changing times that only major rock concerts come close to fulfilling the arena's potential. The building now incorporates an extensive sports complex, including a hotel and a sporting museum, alongside the various stadia and sports halls.

✚ Arrowed from 53D3
✉ Stefánia út, Budapest XIV
☎ For information on sporting events:
   Tourinform (tourist office)
   ☎ 438 8080
🍴 Népstadion (£)
Ⓜ Népstadion
♿ Few
✋ Cheap

ORSZÁGHÁZ (PARLIAMENT) (► 23, TOP TEN)

POSTAMÚZEUM (POSTAL MUSEUM) ✪✪

  52B3

✉ Andrássy út 3, Budapest VI

☎ 269 6838

🕐 Tue–Sun 10–6 (4, Nov to Mar)

🍴 Fesztivál Étterem (£)

Ⓜ Bajcsy-Zsilinszky út, Deák tér

🚌 Bus: 105, red 4

♿ None

💰 Cheap

The Postal Museum boasts an unexpectedly lavish interior

The Postal Museum was formerly a luxurious seven-room private apartment in the once affluent area of Sugarut. The owner's initials 'AS' (Andreás Saxlehner) can be seen all over the house. Most sumptuous of all are the impressive Károly Lotz frescoes on the staircase. Apart from the portable furniture most of the fittings and furniture are original. Attendants will put into operation some of the museum's exhibits. You can even see a section of a pneumatic exchange. An off-beat idea, but together with the other somewhat esoteric museums, it's what makes Budapest such a fascinating city.

RÁKÓCZI ÚT (RÁKÓCZI WAY) ✪

 53C2

✉ Budapest VII

Ⓜ Astoria, Blaha Lujza tér

🚃 Tram: 4, 6

🍴 Orchidea (££)

One of the main shopping areas in Budapest, but with a less Western orientation, Rákóczi út runs from Múzeum körút as far as Baross tér and Keleti pályaudvar. The Verseny Áruház department store, one of the oldest in Budapest, stands at Rákóczi út 12. The Jewish district runs off to the left. Bars, restaurants, well-stocked clothes and electronic shops, and the ubiquitous pizza bars, give the street a rather sleazy appearance. Pay it a visit anyway, if only to experience its ordinary, very down-to-earth atmosphere. This is the real Budapest.

Around Nagykörút (Grand Boulevard)

This is the longest thoroughfare of the city, at 4,114m.

Start at Boráros tér by the Petőfi Bridge heading towards Ferenc körút.

On your left are three large blocks of pre-World War II flats, and between them on Bakats tér the beautiful spired Ferencváros Parish Church.

Carry on up Ferenc körút to Üllői út and the Museum of Applied Arts (➤ 65). Crossing Üllői út, on your right is the Corvin Cinema, once the headquarters of armed resistance during the 1956 Uprising. Now you're on Jósef körút. On your way to Rákóczi tér, on the right look out for the impressive War Memorial.

Rákóczi tér, always a colourful area, still is, but in a rather seedy way.

Further on up the tree-lined boulevard, on the right is Blaha Lujza tér, one of the central squares in the city. Cross Rákóczi út, and make for the most famous café in Hungary – Café New York on the right. Now you're on Erzsébet körút. The Grand Hotel Royal is on your right. A short walk further on is Teréz körút with the magnificent Academy of Music (➤ 77).

On the right where Andrássy út joins the Oktogon is the Florentine copy of Palazzo Strozzi, with its richly decorated wedding hall.

A little further on, with the Hotel Béke Radisson on the right, you arrive at Nyugati tér with the finely restored Western Railway Station (➤ 69). Crossing Szent István körút, the corner is presided over by a daunting block of flats. Perhaps you are footsore by now, but keep going. On your right, at Szent István körút, is the Vígszínház theatre. A short walk past the block of flats on the right, nicknamed the 'electric switch building' because its square white stones bring modern switches to mind, and you arrive at Margaret Bridge and the Danube.

Distance
4km

Time
4–5 hours, 6 hours with stops

Start point
Boráros tér
🚇 South of Square 52B1
🚊 Tram: 2

End point
Margit hid (Margaret Bridge)
🚇 Arrowed from 52A5
🚊 Tram: 2

Lunch
New York
✉ Erzsébet Körút 9–11
☎ 322 3849

Café New York, where Hungary's literati and glitterati once met

71

➕ 52A4
📧 Budapest V
🍴 Don Pepe Pizzeria (£)
🚇 Kossuth tér
🚌 Tram: 2; bus: 15
♿ None
↔ Országház (Parliament, ► 23), Szent István Bazilika (St Stephen's Basilica, ► 24)

The Post Office Savings Bank is a synthesis of simplicity and ornamental folk art

SZABADSÁG TÉR (LIBERTY SQUARE) ✪✪✪

This vast open space in the city centre between the Parliament building and St Stephen's Basilica was laid out by Antal Paloczy in 1902. The site was once occupied by a huge military barracks called Neugebäude, which gave rise to the square and neighbourhood after it was pulled down. Among the different palaces, one art-nouveau building, the American Embassy, is very prominent. The statue in front of the building is of the US General, Harry Hill Bandholtz. An officer of the entente peace-keeping force in 1919, he saved the treasures of the National Museum by sealing its doors with censorship seals. These bore the US Coat of Arms and so deterred the Romanian soldiers from plundering the museum. Also on the square and near by are the headquarters of Hungarian television, the Ministry of Agriculture, the Ethnographical Museum, and the Post Office Savings Bank.

SZENT ISTVÁN BAZILIKA (ST STEPHEN'S BASILICA)
(► 24, TOP TEN)

SZÉPMŰVÉSZETI MÚZEUM (FINE ARTS MUSEUM)
(► 25, TOP TEN)

Inner City

This walk in downtown Pest serves as an introduction to the commercial and cultural heart of the city.

Start at Kossuth Lajos tér outside the magnificent Parliament (➤ 23). With your back to the Parliament, turn right down Nádor utca towards Szabadság tér, a hidden gem of the city.

At 8–9 is the stately bulk of the Hungarian National Bank. On the southwest corner towards the square is the figure of Hamlet holding poor Yorik's skull.

Return to Nádor utca and turn right towards József Attila utca. Before reaching it, turn right into Roosevelt tér.

At the northern end is the Hungarian Academy of Sciences (➤ 67), the first neo-Renaissance building in the city, built between 1862 and 1864. Also on the square is Gresham Palace, a richly ornate art-nouveau building.

Back on Nádor utca, turn right. You come to the intersection with József Attila utca, with its incessant flow of traffic. Cross it and head straight on to József nádor tér, once one of the most attractive squares in the city before the advent of the motor car.

Occupying the square is the Romantic-style Postabank Headquarters; Gross House, a neo-classical block of flats; and the Central European University, a classical *chef d'oeuvre*.

Leave József nádor tér and make for Bécsi utca. Turn right, and walk down to Vörösmarty tér, a pleasant and restful square.

At No 7 is the famous Gerbeaud pastry shop – so stop for a snack.

Walk to the far side to Váci utca (➤ 77), the smartest shopping street in town. If you can resist the shops, continue under the subway towards the Central Market Hall on Vámház körút.

The 19th-century Market Hall (➤ 76) is a place to wander or have a snack or beer at one of the small upstairs bars.

Gresham Palace, lavish in its heyday and now being restored

Distance
Approximately 3km

Time
2 hours, half a day with stops

Start point
Kossuth Lajos tér
52A5
M Kossuth Lajos tér

End point
Central Market Hall (Vásárcsarnok)
53C1
Tram: 2, 47, 49; trolley bus: 83

Lunch
Fatál (£)
 Váci utca 67
266 2607

75B1

✉ Bordered by Dózsa
György út, Ajósi Dürer
sor, Hermina út and a
railway embankment,
Budapest XIV

🅟 Park: open access

🍴 Robinson (££)

Ⓢ Széchenyi fürdő

🚌 Bus: 20,30,105, red 4;
trolley bus: 70, 72, 75, 79

Állatkert

🚩 75A4

✉ Állatkerti körút 6–12

☎ 343 6075

🅟 9–7 (5, Sep–Apr)

💰 Cheap

Fővárosi Nagycirkusz

🚩 75B4

✉ Állatkerti körút 12

☎ 343 8300

🅟 Perfomances: Mon, Thu,
Fri 3PM, Sat 10AM, 3PM,
7PM, Sun 10AM, 3PM

💰 Cheap

Vidámpark

🚩 75B4

✉ Állatkerti körút 14–16

☎ 343 0996

🅟 Daily 10–8 (6, Oct–Mar)

💰 Free

Széchenyi Gyógyfürdő

🚩 75B3

✉ Állatkerti körút 11

☎ 321 0310

🅟 Daily 6AM–7PM (5PM, Oct
to Apr, Sat, Sun)

💰 Cheap

*Chess, a favourite past-
time with Hungarian
spa-bathers*

VÁROSLIGET (CITY PARK) ✪✪✪

The City Park is the biggest of its kind in Budapest, where you can find just about every form of entertainment for children, as well as tranquillity for the adults. Standing on an island in the boating lake is the fairy-tale Vajdahunyad Vár (Castle), modelled on a Transylvanian castle. The Állatkert (Zoo, ➤ 108) is a perennial favourite with children, especially the 'Animal Kindergarten' where newly born animals are kept. Next to the Zoo is the Fővárosi Nagycirkusz (Municipal Circus, ➤ 108), a must for the kids. The Vidámpark (Amusement Park, ➤ 108) is also very popular, though rather jaded looking. Here you'll find a carousel, roller-coaster, Ferris wheel, an enchanted castle, and a slot-machine hall.

The Széchenyi Gyógyfürdő (thermal baths) are opposite the circus. The largest of its kind in Europe, it is visited by an astonishing 2 million people annually. One wonders if they come to bathe in the pools and medicinal baths, or to admire the building's beautiful art-nouveau mosaic, as well as its lavish fittings and furnishings. Here you'll see visitors playing chess on floating cork chess-boards while relaxing in the thermal pools. You can study their games from the lively restaurant there.

Towards the southwest corner of the park at Városligeti körút 11 is the Közlekedési Múzeum (Transport Museum,

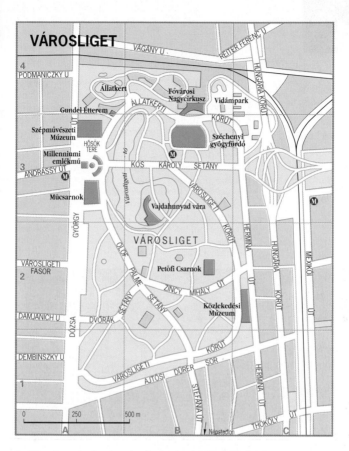

VÁROSLIGET

PODMANICZKY U.
VÁGÁNY U.
REITER FERENC U.
HUNGÁRIA KÖRÚT
Állatkert
Fővárosi Nagycirkusz
Vidámpark
Gundel Étterem
ÁLLATKERTI
KÖRÚT
Szépművészeti Múzeum
HŐSÖK TERE
Széchenyi gyógyfürdő
Millenniumi emlékmű
ANDRÁSSY ÚT
KÓS KÁROLY SÉTÁNY
Műcsarnok
Városligeti tó
VÁROSLIGETI KÖRÚT
Vajdahunyad vára
HERMINA
HUNGÁRIA KÖRÚT
MEXIKÓI
GYÖRGY
VÁROSLIGET
VÁROSLIGETI FASOR
OLOF PALME SÉTÁNY
Petőfi Csarnok
ZICHY MIHÁLY ÚT
DAMJANICH U.
DÓZSA
DVORÁK SÉTÁNY
Közlekedési Múzeum
DEMBINSZKY U.
VÁROSLIGETI AJTÓSI DÜRER SOR
KÖRÚT
HERMINA ÚT
STEFÁNIA ÚT
THÖKÖLY ÚT
0   250   500 m
A   B   Népstadion   C

➤ 65) and near by the charming Garden for the Blind. Of interest also is **Petőfi Csarnok** (Hall), once the site of an exhibition centre, but now the bastion of Hungarian rock and pop music. It also plays host to a flea market, theatre for children, roller-skating club, and on Saturday evenings the Csillagfeny Disco. This is *the* venue for the young and trendy. In summer there's also an open-air cinema.

Did you know ?

The elephants in Budapest's zoo share their house with a recently discovered rare fresco.

Közlekedési Múzeum
➕ 75C2
✉ Városliget körút 11
☎ 343 0565
🕐 May–Sep, Tue–Fri 10–5, Sat, Sun 10–6; Oct–Apr Tue–Fri 10–4, Sat, Sun 10–5
💳 Cheap

Petőfi Csarnok
➕ 75B2
✉ Zichy Mihály út 14
☎ 343 4327
🕐 Flea market Sat AM

75

+ 53C1
✉ Fővám körút 1–3,
  Budapest IX
☎ 218 5322
🕐 Mon 6AM–5PM, Tue–Fri
  6AM–6PM, Sat 6AM–4PM.
  Closed Sun
🍴 Market hall food bars (£)
🚃 Tram: 2, 47, 49; trolley
  bus: 83
♿ Good
👌 Free
↔ Váci utca (➤ 77)

*The vast indoor Central
Market*

VÁSÁRCSARNOK (CENTRAL MARKET HALL) ✪✪✪

The Central Market is all you could ever wish of an old
market place – full of the aromas of fresh vegetables, fish,
hung sausages, mountainous cheeses, flowers, and the
beauty of folk art handicrafts – traditional lacework,
jewellery and woodcrafts. And on the lower floor is the
Pick Market, a mingling of the modern supermarket and
the bargain-basement stall. In past days laden barges
sailed to its doors. Above one of its entrances a notice
reads: 'Tunnel into the Central Market'. Its lofty iron-girder
construction gives the market a grandiloquent atmosphere
but also a sense of sober commercial pragmatism. The
best bargain is a beer and snack at one of the small bars
on the upper floor. This market is special for its authentic
flavour of Hungarian life.

VÖRÖSMARTY TÉR (SQUARE) AND VÁCI UTCA (STREET) ⊕⊕

Named after the 19th-century Romantic poet, Mihály Vörösmarty (1800–55), the square is a real delight. The poet's monument stands in the centre. On the north side, at No 7, is the famous Gerbeaud pastry shop – just the place for a tasty snack. Váci utca, on the far side of the square, is Budapest's premier shopping street. The shopping here is small scale with big brand names – Estée Lauder, Adidas etc. The entire street is pedestrianised but, attractive as it is, it looks much like any European pedestrianised shopping area.

🕇 52A3
✉ Budapest V
🍴 Resti (£)
Ⓜ Metro Vörösmarty tér
🚋 Tram: 2
↔ Orságház (Parliament, ► 23), Szent István Bazilika (St Stephen's Basilica, ► 24)

The majestic Walcker organ

ZENEAKADÉMIA (ACADEMY OF MUSIC) ⊕⊕

The building was completed in 1907, and its official name is something of a mouthful: Liszt Ferenc Zeneművészeti Főiskola. The first president was the great Franz Liszt himself (a bronze statue of him stands above the main entrance), and the first director was Ferenc Erkel. The main hall seats 1,200, and is dominated by the magnificent Walcker organ. On each side of the organ there are inscriptions in Latin: *Sursum Corda* (Raise Your Hearts) on the left; and *Favete Linguis* (Shut Up, or Be Quiet) on the right. A beautiful art-nouveau building, the Academy is the centre of Budapest's musical life.

🕇 53C4
✉ Liszt Ferenc tér 8, Budapest VI
☎ 341 4788
🕐 From 10AM to performance end
🍴 Művész (£)
Ⓜ Oktogon
🚋 Tram: 4, 6
♿ None
🎫 Free

Excursions from the City

Budapest has much to offer beyond the city limits. To the north is the popular Danube Bend, the most beautiful stretch of the river in Hungary where it turns sharply between the Pilis and Börzsöny hills.

Also north is the village of Hollókö, now on UNESCO's World Heritage list. Other picturesque towns and villages are within a short drive, like Esztergom, once the country's capital; or Szentendre, with its relaxed cultural atmosphere; and Visegrád, steeped in history and rural heritage. If you are in search of a day by the water, but away from the Danube, head southwest to the breathtaking Lake Balaton. Note that the traffic out of the city can be particularly heavy on Fridays, when many Pestians migrate to the countryside.

> *'The consequences of the last 1,000 years, the surviving architectural, cultural, and other values in this country, show us the timeless value and influence of St István's legacy'*
>
> OTTO HAPSBURG, MEP
> World Heritage, Hungary

An elegant Serbian cross stands outside a church in Szentendre

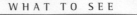

EXCURSIONS

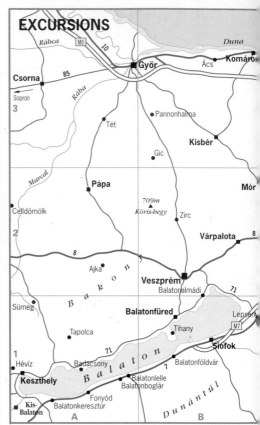

The imposing walls of Eger Castle

✚ Arrowed from 81D3

🚍 Hourly return service from Budapest. By car: 128km, M3

ℹ Dobó István tér, Eger
☎ 321 807

Serbian church

✉ Vitkovics Mihaly utca 30

🕐 10–4, Tue–Sun

🍴 Gyros (££)

♿ None

💷 Free

EGER ⭐⭐⭐

Famous for its Bull's Blood red wine (Egri Bikver), this historic baroque city played a central role in the attempt to overthrow the Austrian Hapsburgs early in the 18th century. The Austrians destroyed much of the town, and what we see today was built by Eger's bishops and archbishops in the late 18th century. The beautiful palaces and churches are some of Hungary's finest examples of Copf architecture, a transitional style between late baroque and neo-classical found only in central Europe.

Some of the city's finest buildings and sights can be found along Kossuth Lajos utca, including the baroque County Hall, the magnificent Provost's House, the 18th-century Franciscan church on the site of a mosque and the former Orthodox synagogue.

Off Dobó utca, István Dobó tér is the main square of the city. Largely paved with formal gardens, its centrepiece

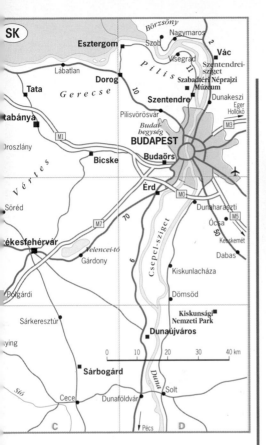

SK

Börzsöny

Esztergom · Szob · Nagymaros

Vác

Lábatlan · Visegrád · Szentendrei-sziget

Dorog · Szabadtéri Néprajzi Múzeum

Tata · Gerecse · Szentendre · Dunakeszi

Eger Hollókő

tabánya · Pilisvörösvár

M1 · Budai-hegység · BUDAPEST · M3

Oroszlány

Bicske · Budaörs

Vértes

Érd · M0

Söréd · Dunaharaszti · M5

M7 · 70 · Ócsa · 50

ékesfehérvár · Kecskemét

Velencei-tó · Dabas

Gárdony · 6

Pólgárdi · Kiskunlacháza

Dömsöd

Sárkeresztúr · Kiskunsági Nemzeti Park

Dunaújváros

ying

0 10 20 30 40 km

Sárbogárd

Stó · Duna

Cece · Dunaföldvár · Solt

C · D · Pécs

Inside Eger's 18th-century Minorite church

is the magnificent statue celebrating the heroic siege of 2,000 Hungarians against an overwhelming number of Turks. This is also site of the 8th-century Minorite church, considered one of the most beautiful baroque buildings in Hungary. The entrance features a statue of Dobo and beautiful heroic sculptures depicting the battle against the Turks. The carved wood furnishing inside is breathtaking. Another must is the Greek Orthodox **Serbian church**, which boasts the largest iconostasis in Hungary. Set against a cool whitewashed wall, its elaborate intricacy is spellbinding. Flanking the iconostasis is other richly decorated ecclesiastical craftwork.

Constructed in the 13th century after the Mongol invasion, imposing **Eger Vár** (Castle) has often been at the forefront of Hungary's long and turbulent history. Inside are the foundations of St John's Cathedral, which was destroyed by the Turks. Models and drawings of the

Eger Vár

✚ Arrowed from 81D3

✉ Vár 1

☎ 312 744

🕐 1 Nov–28 Feb 9–5; 1 Apr–30 Sep 9–6; Mar, Oct 8–6. Museum: 9–3 Nov 1–Feb 28; 9–5 Mar 1–Sept 30; closed Mon

🍴 Imola Café (£)

♿ None

💷 Cheap

Below: *Esztergom Cathedral, dwarfing the town below*

cathedral in the Istvan Dobó Museum show how it once looked. The museum is named after the national hero who led the resistance to the Turks in 1552. Worth seeing are the underground casemates, situated below the castle, which were hewn from solid rock. In the shadow of the castle stands the northernmost Turkish minaret in Europe. Rising to a height of 40m with a cross, you can climb the cramped 100 spiral steps to the top for marvellous views over the town.

After all the sightseeing, the quiet and restful Archbishop's Garden, once the private reserve of papal princes, is the place to relax. Or you could swim in its open-air and covered pools, or take a dip in one of its thermal baths dating from Turkish times.

ESZTERGOM ✪✪✪

Birthplace of King Stephen I, this is one of Hungary's most historically important and fascinating cities. Its history dates back to Roman times when one of its most renowned visitors, Marcus Aurelius, camped here. Sadly, much of the original city was destroyed by the Turks in 1543. All the same, it boasts some of Hungary's most prestigious buildings, the most impressive of which is the Basilika, Hungary's largest cathedral. Little remains of the medieval building, with the present neo-classical structure dating from the early 19th century. The Bakócz Chapel is by far the most dominant feature in this sumptuously decorated building. The white marble altar is the work of Florentine craftsmen and was designed by Andreas Ferrucci in 1519. With its many priceless medieval objects,

---

✚ 81D3

🚌 Bus: Frequent service from Budapest's Árpád híd bus station. By car: 66km, route 11

🚆 Regular service from Nyugati Railway Station

ℹ️ Gran Tours ✉️ Széchenyi tér 25, Esztergom ☎ (33) 417 052

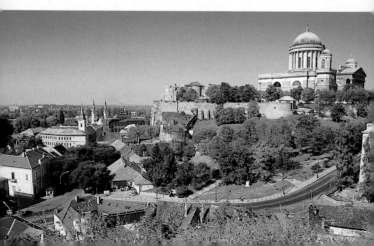

including the 13th-century Hungarian Coronation Cross, the treasury is also resting place of Cardinal Mindszenty, the cathedral's most famous clergyman. Beside the basilica is the Vár Múzeum (Castle Museum), housing the fascinating remains of the former Royal Palace.

Don't miss the Keresztény Múzeum (Christian Museum), containing the best collection of medieval religious art in Hungary, and also works by Italian masters Duccio, Lorenzo di Credi and Gionvanni di Paola. Since the Danube is such a dominant feature of the town, there's the Duna Múzeum (Danube Museum) to help you understand its evolution. Although most of the captions are in Hungarian, this doesn't lessen the impact of the exhibition.

Below: *the simple styling of Győr's Cathedral*

GYŐR ✪✪

The large industrial centre of Győr (pronounced 'jyeur'), is usually missed off the tourists' map. But standing in the charming old centre of the town, you'd hardly know there's any industry here at all. Start at Bécsi kapu tér (Vienna Gate Square), where you'll find an array of interesting sites, including the enchanting Carmelite church built in 1725 and recently renovated, and several fine baroque palaces. Káptalandomb (Chapter Hill), the oldest part of Győr, is dominated by a large baroque cathedral. Originally Romanesque, most of its interior, with fine ceiling frescoes, dates from the 17th and 18th centuries. On nearby Széchenyi tér is St Ignatius Church built in 1641, and the finest church in Győr with a superb pulpit, pews and ceiling frescoes.

About 20km southeast of Győr is the splendid 11th-century Pannonhalma Abbey. Built like a fortress, it occupies a strategic position on St Martin's Mount, its architects must have foreseen the turbulent history that lay ahead: the devastating Mongul invasion which it miraculously survived; then the Turkish occupation when it became part of the frontier fortifications. Surprisingly, the Turks, who eventually captured it, didn't 'convert' the monastery into a mosque, but shared it with the Hungarian Christians. In the 18th century it became a teacher-training and theological college, and thereafter experienced a period of relative peace, even during World War II, when it became one of the most modern boarding schools in the country. Today the church resounds with the chant *pro stabilite regni nostri* ('for the stability of our realm').

81A3
Bus: Hourly from Budapest
Regular services from Déli and Keleti Railway Stations (2 hours), ☎ Fovinform (1) 317 1173 for information on train and bus times (24 hour service). By car: 123km, M1
Tourinform ✉ Árpád út 32 Győr ☎ (96) 311 771

Tour Around Lake Balaton

Coach Tour Operator
Cityrama
☎ (1) 302 4382/332 5344

Departs
Apr–Oct, Tue, Sat 9AM

Duration
9 hours

Start/end point
Budapest
✛ 81D3

Price
Moderate

Lunch
Pál Csárda, Tihany

Europe's largest freshwater lake, known as 'The Sea of the Hungarians', covers nearly 600sq m and is a tourist paradise. The hills on the northern shore are cultivated with vineyards, while the southern shore has excellent beaches and shallow water. The plentiful resorts focus on a range of watersports and cycling, and offer interesting sights, shopping and particularly good restaurants and cafés.

The coach travels along the M7 and route 71 to Balatonfüred.

This stop is the lake's oldest resort and spa, with a sanatorium known as the 'Mecca of those with heart diseases'. An elegant town, it has an easy going atmosphere and is relatively uncommercialised.

After a walk round Balatonfüred you board the coach and travel on to the peninsula town of Tihany.

Tihany's nature reserve is the first of its kind in Hungary and is home to a huge variety of wildlife. A visit to the Benedictine monastery is next. This fascinating abbey, built in 1055, houses the famous Latin Charter, the first written relic of the Hungarian language.

After lunch you board a ferry for a ride across the lake. On your return there is wine tasting at one of the hotels.

Sunset over yachts in the marina at Balatonfüred, on the shores of Lake Balaton

HÉVÍZ ✪✪

For spas and 'taking the waters', Hévíz is one of the best sites in Europe. Here you'll find Gyógy-tó, Europe's largest thermal lake, or natural swimming pool if you prefer. For centuries the people of this area used the warm mineral water for a variety of purposes: first as a tannery in the Middle Ages (one wonders how it ever recovered), and later for curative purposes. The lake derives its name from Count György Festetics of Keszthely, who developed the lake as a private resort in 1795; but it really only became popular at the end of the 19th century. The lake itself has a surface of almost 5ha in the Parkerdő (Park Forest), and for most of the year it's covered with beautiful pink-and-white water lilies, making it quite an astonishing sight. The temperature averages 33°C and never drops below 26°C, thus allowing bathing throughout the year – that's if you can bear getting out in sub-zero temperatures during the winter. The spring is a crater some 40m deep which produces around 80 million litres of warm water a day. The water and mud on the bottom are slightly radioactive and are recommended for locomotive and nervous ailments. You can find the lake's *fin de siècle* central pavilion by walking over a covered bridge. Here catwalks and piers offer protected bathing, as also do the rafts and anchors further out in the lake. A couple of piers along the shore are especially for sunbathing.

🚏 80A1

🚌 Bus: About five a day from Budapest. By car: 200km, M7, Route 71, Route 76

ℹ️ Hévíz Tourist ☎ (83) 341 348; Zalatour ☎ (83) 341 048 – both on Rákóczi utca, Hévíz

A perfect day at Hévíz's natural thermal lake

Touring the Danube Bend

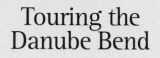

Coach Tour Operator
Cityrama
☎ (1) 302 4382/332 5344

Departs
Apr–Nov, Wed–Fri, Sun 9AM

Duration
10 hours

Start/End point
Budapest
✚ 81D3

Price
Moderate

Lunch
In Visegrád

Commanding view of the Danube Bend from the fortress town of Visegrád

Exceptionally rich in attractive landscapes, picturesque towns and monuments, the Danube Bend occupies around 20km of the river. The west–east direction of the river turns suddenly south at Zebegény, then east, then north at Visegrád, then south again. Before Budapest, the river breaks into two arms encompassing the Szentendre Island. Between the 1st and the 5th centuries, this part of the river formed the fortified border of the Roman Empire, called the Limes. Deservedly a popular tourist area, it is one of the most enchanting and captivating parts of Hungary.

The Danube Bend coach excursion takes you along Route 11 to Visegrád (➤ 90), the first stop.

The visit includes a trip to the former Royal Residence, one of the most impressive remains of Visegrád's Golden Age before and during the reign of Matthias Corvinus. Its location offers spectacular views of the Danube.

The coach then follows the river through Dömös along the river to Esztergom (➤ 82).

Esztergom is famous for being, amongst other things, the seat of the Hungarian Catholic Church. It was a royal capital until the 13th century, and St Stephen was crowned here. A visit to the cathedral, Hungary's largest church, is included in the tour.

On to Szentendre (➤ 89) and a guided walk round the baroque artists' village.

Work from the Artists' Colony, old and new, can be seen here, including one of the most prodigious collections of ceramics in Hungary, housed in the Margit Kovács Museum.

The tour can then be completed by a return trip to Budapest by boat along the Danube.

KECSKEMÉT ✪✪

Known as the Garden City of Hungary for the million fruit trees in the surrounding area, Kecskemét is almost at the geographical centre of Hungary, close to the beautiful Kiskunság National Park in the heart of the puszta, the Great Plain. It is a leafy, clean city, famous for its apricots, and especially its potent apricot brandy, *barackpálinka*.

One of the city's best sights is the fine Naiv Müvészek Múseum (Museum of Naïve Art) in the Stork House, built in 1730. The art gallery directly below offers original paintings for sale which are almost as good as the ones on display in the museum.

The sights centre around three main squares, and around Kossuth tér and Szabadsag tér are some of the most interesting, including the imposing Town Hall, built in 1897 and featuring a carillon that plays on the hour, every hour. Facing the Town Hall, though shrouded by bushes, is the József Katona Memorial commemorating the death of a young playwright who unfortunately dropped dead of a heart attack there in 1830. On either side of the Town Hall are two fine churches, the neo-classical Great Church and the older Church of St Nicholas, dating in part from the 13th century. On Két templom köz, directly behind the hall, stands the Kodály Institute of Music Education, which occupies an old baroque monastery. Near by on Katona József tér is the magnificent József Katona Theatre, in front of which stands a fine baroque statue of the Trinity .

◆ Arrowed from 81D2
◻ Regular service from Budapest-Nyugat Railway Station
◻ Hourly service from Budapest. By car: 8km, M5
ℹ Tourinform, Kossuth Lajos téri, Kecskemét ☎ (76) 481 065; or Pusztatourist, Szabadság tér 2, Kecskemét ☎ (76) 483 493

The sweeping interior of Kecskemét Town Hall

Arrowed from 81D1

About 10 trains a day from Budapest-Déli Station. By car: 230km, route 6

Tourinform, Szénchenyi tér 9, Pécs ☎ (72) 213 315

One of Pécs's mosques, a legacy of the Turkish invasion

PÉCS ✪✪✪

This large and historical city is beautifully located on the southern slopes of the Mecsek Hills between the Danube and Drava rivers. It is the home of Zsolnay porcelain and Pannonvin sparkling wine. In 1009 Stephen I, Hungary's first king, made Pécs a bishopric. The invading Turks left some of their greatest monuments here in the city – especially mosques – and these, together with an impressive synagogue, numerous museums and a lively student atmosphere, make it worth a visit. Be sure not to miss the Régészeti Múzeum (Archaeological Museum) on Széchenyi tér. Not only is it well designed, but its exhibits,

from prehistory up to the Magyar Conquest, offer a unique and fascinating perspective on this often turbulent period of the country's history. The Bazilika, while not the most attractive church in itself, is worth a brief visit. Largely rebuilt in neo-Romanesque style in 1881, its 11th-century crypt is its only original feature. Káptalan utca is almost totally dominated by a number of museums, many displaying the works of local artists. The Zsolnay Porcelain Museum features beautiful art-nouveau and art deco works from the 19th century. Before leaving Pécs, you should take a stroll in the Mecsek Hills which offer lovely walks and have trail signs in abundance. The walking is not arduous, so head straight to the top for the splendid panoramic views.

81C2

Regularly from Budapest's Erzsébet tér Station. By car: 66km, route 70

Regularly from Budapest-Déli station

Tourinform, Városház tér, Székesfehérvár ☎ (22) 312 818

SZÉKESFEHÉRVÁR ✪✪

With its tongue-twisting and virtually unpronounceable name, this is considered the oldest town in Hungary, settled by the 9th-century Magyar chieftain Árpád. Its name means 'seat of the white castle' – 'seat' being the royal capital, and 'white' the king's colour. An astonishing 36 kings of medieval Hungary were crowned in the 12th-century Royal Basilica, and 15 were buried in its crypt. The basilica's foundations lie in the Romkert (Garden of Ruins). In the old town is Városház tér, a good base for visiting sights like the grand old Town Hall. Fő utca offers several interesting sights: the daunting Bishop's Palace and beautiful Cistercian church; the István Király Museum with archaeological and folk art exhibitions; and the Black Eagle Museum with its splendid rococo furnishings.

SZENTENDRE ●●●

Szentendre lies in a beautiful vale of hills beside the Danube. Founded in the 11th century, it takes its name from the guardian angel of its church, Andras (Endre). In the 14th century it became a royal estate, but 150 years of Turkish occupation followed, at the end of which the town was virtually deserted. It was later settled by rich craftsmen and merchants, but the town again went into decline. But much is still intact, and it's worth starting your visit on Fő tér (Main Square), with its huddled houses and alleyways like Jeno Dumsta utca and Bogdani utca, the main shopping and restaurant area. The Memorial Cross in the middle of the square was erected in thanks for the end of the Black Death by the Privileged Merchants' Company in 1763.

Near by on Fő körút is the Orthodox Episcopal Church, also known as Beograda. Built between 1756–1764, its baroque architecture houses a lavishly ornamented and decorated interior. Apparently one of its steeples had to be rebuilt several times. The splendid Margit Kovács Museum is one of the most delightful galleries in Szentendre and houses the works of the famous ceramicist after whom it is named. For superb views of Szentendre, and a pleasant walk as well, take a stroll up to Templom tér, the highest point of the town, where a narrow cobbled lane leads up to the square. From here you'll be treated to a cavalcade of russet roof tiles sloping down to the Danube, interrupted occasionally by dots of green gardens. No trip to the town of Szentendre would be complete without a visit to the fascinating Szabadadtéri Néprajzi Muzeum, known as the Hungarian 'Skansen', which was opened in 1974. Originals of houses, buildings and machines were taken apart then reassembled here to represent Hungarian national architecture.

81D3

By car: 20km, route 11

By boat and coach: Departure 2:30 Tue–Sun, Mar–Oct; 10 Tue, Fri ,Sun Nov–Mar (return by coach). Bookings: Cityrama ☎ 302 4382

Szentendre; Dumtsa Jenő ut ☎ 317 965

The thatched Village Museum is a delightful feature of Szentendre

🕂 81D3

🚌 Regular return service from Budapest's Árpád Bridge station. By car: 40km, route 11

🚉 Take train to Szob (24 daily) from Budapest-Nyugati station. Get off at Nagymaros-Visegrád and take a ferry across to Visegrád

🚢 Mahart hydrofoil links Budapest and Esztergom via Visegrád twice a day 8AM, 2:10PM (late May–early Sep)

ℹ️ Sütő ut 2, Budapest ☎ (1) 438 8080

The ruins of the Royal Palace in Visegrád

VISEGRÁD ✪✪

Offering magnificent views of the Danube, Visegrád (a Slav name meaning 'lofty fortress') lies on the river's abrupt loop between the Pilis and Börzsöny Hills. The town dates from Roman times when the Danube formed the border of the Roman Empire. After the Mongul invasion, the Hungarian kings built the imposing Citadel, a formidable fortification, dominating the hilltop above Solomon's Tower. During the Turkish occupation Visegrád was virtually destroyed, and later the Hapsburgs blew up the citadel to prevent its use by Hungarian independence fighters. Now being restored, the best way to reach it is by the excellent hiking trails following signposts marked 'Fellegvár', starting from behind the Catholic church.

The other major sight worth looking at in Visegrád is the 14-century Royal Palace. Largely destroyed by the Hapsburgs in 1702, the building has been under excavation since 1934. Highlights here include the red-marbled Hercules Fountain in the Gothic courtyard and the Lion Fountain.

Where To...

Above: *richly carved detail on St Stephen's Basilica*
Right: *quirky exhibit in the Museum of Catering*

Buda

Prices

Though prices are steadily increasing, eating out in Budapest is, by western standards, relatively inexpensive.

Prices are approximate based upon an average three-course meal for one, without drinks or service (a bottle of wine will make little difference to the bill, and service is sometimes included) – otherwise tip to 10–15 per cent:

£ = under 3,000HUF
££ = 3,000–6,000HUF
£££ = over 6,000HUF

Les Amis (£)

This is a small, friendly place tucked away in a quiet street and serving a limited menu, but only because of its size.

✉ Rómer Floóris utca 12, Budapest II ☎ 315 1643 🕒 Lunch, dinner. Closed Sun

Aranykaviár (££)

There is no need to point out that this restaurant specialises in caviar – and reputedly the best quality, But if caviar is not to your liking, there are a host of other Russian specialities on the menu.

✉ Ostrom utca 19, Budapest I ☎ 201 6737 🕒 Lunch, dinner

Café Pierrot Restaurant (££)

Hungarian specialities with an international flavour in the Castle district. It also has an extensive vegetarian menu. Piano music in the evenings.

✉ Fortuna ucta 14, Budapest I ☎ 375 6971 🕒 Lunch, dinner

Dominican Restaurant (££)

Although this is the restaurant of the Hilton Hotel, it's not really that pricey. The hotel's setting in the picturesque Buda Castle District makes it an attractive place to eat if you are in the area. All the same, this is a hotel restaurant, resplendently ordinary with a full menu and wine list.

✉ Hess András tér 1–3, Budapest 1 ☎ 488 6757

Duna Restaurant (££)

The famous Gellért Hotel's restaurant offers views of the Danube that are as appetising as the food. Pikeperch dishes and veal Gellért-style are among the

many house specialities on offer.

✉ Gellért tér 1, Budapest XI ☎ 466 5103 🕒 Lunch, dinner. Closed Sun

Hong Kong Pearl Garden (££)

This excellent Chinese restaurant at the Buda end of Margaret Bridge offers a full menu, varied wine list and a selection of good Hungarian and international beers.

✉ Margit körút 2, Budapest II ☎ 212 3131/3948 🕒 Lunch, dinner

Kasca (££)

Duck is the speciality (as the name in Hungarian suggests), but the restaurant also serves other dishes. Live piano/violin music in the evenings.

✉ Főutca 75, Budapest I ☎ 201 9992 🕒 Lunch, dinner. Dinner only Sat, Sun

Kéhli (££)

This is an authentic Hungarian restaurant catering for a mainly local clientele. It can become busy and you may need to book a place in the main dining area, which features a gypsy band.

✉ Mókus utca 22, Budapest III ☎ 250 4241 🕒 Mon–Sun dinner only; Sat–Sun lunch, dinner

Kerék (£)

Traditional, old-established small restaurant in Old Buda with a good reputation. Live music in the evenings. Small courtyard.

✉ Bécsi út 103, Budapest III ☎ 250 4261

Kikelet (£)

A basic eatery offering good grills and salads at very

reasonable prices in a relaxed and informal atmosphere.

✉ **Fillér utca 85, Budapest II** ☎ **212 5444** 🕓 **Lunch, dinner**

Kisbuda Gyöngye (££)

This restaurant is very Hungarian, magnificently styled in turn-of-the-century bourgeois affectation, with a languorous but genial piano-violin duo setting the mood. The place is melodically atmospheric with a rich and varied menu, where a Bull's Blood red wine is an ideal accompaniment.

✉ **Kenyeres út 34, Budapest III** ☎ **368 6402** 🕓 **Lunch, dinner. Closed Sun**

Makk Hetes (£)

Small, popular, local family-run restaurant. There is outside seating in the summer.

✉ **Némnetvölgyi út 56, Budapest XII** ☎ **355 7330**

Náncsi Néni (££)

This restuarant is an oasis of Hungarian cooking, offering a warm atmosphere and large menu. Just one of the recommendation is 'Kamermayer's Delight' (turkey breast steeped in garlic milk and coated in ground walnuts).

✉ **Ördögárok út 80, Budapest II** ☎ **397 2742** 🕓 **Lunch, dinner**

Orient Express (£)

It doesn't take its name from that vintage express for nothing. Occupying an old refurbished train carriage, the restaurant is situated next to Déli Station and serves good Hungarian and international cuisine.

✉ **Vérmező út, Budapest I** ☎ **213 0122** 🕓 **Lunch, dinner**

Remiz (£)

Specialising in grilled dishes, this restaurant is popular for its secluded garden and relaxed barbecue-style atmosphere.

✉ **Budakeszi út 5, Budapest II** ☎ **275 1396** 🕓 **Lunch, dinner**

Ressaikos (£)

Here a Greek chef and Greek wines are complemented with live bouzouki music Thursday, Friday and Saturday. The restaurant serves shark steak and goat meat as well as traditional dishes.

✉ **Apor Péter utca 1, Budapest I** ☎ **212 1612** 🕓 **Lunch, dinner**

Rivalda (£££)

The restaurant has a theatrically inspired décor, hence the name. The Castle Theatre is next door. Pleasant jazz piano music in the evenings.

✉ **Színház utca 5–9, Budapest I** ☎ **489 0236** 🕓 **Lunch, dinner**

Római Party Étterem (£)

This small, self-service restaurant along the Danube has no pretensions, prices that are hard to beat, but a good and varied menu all the same.

✉ **Római Part 53, Budapest III** 🕓 **Daily 10–6**

Seoul House (£)

A Korean restaurant, Seoul House serves authentic *kimchee*, and excellent beef dishes in a very pleasant and friendly atmosphere.

✉ **Fő utca 8, Budapest I** ☎ **201 7452** 🕓 **Lunch, dinner. Closed Sun**

Spoilt for Choice

With increasing numbers of foreign visitors, there is a corresponding diversity of places to eat in the city. There are over 1,000 restaurants in Budapest, offering a varied range of traditional Hungarian and international cuisines at a wide range of prices. Among these are Chinese, Korean, Thai, Indian, Iranian, Italian, Tex-Mex and a growing number of familiar fast-food outlets. You will also find a selection of vegetarian and even kosher places.

What to Eat

The most familiar Hungarian dish is, of course, goulash – a thick, substantial soup (not stew), based on beef, potatoes and onions, flavoured with the all-important paprika. You should also try the local *pörkölt* (stew) and goose liver – fried or grilled, hot or cold. Other specialities include sweet and salty pasta, with unusual offerings such as *túrós csúsza* (pasta with curd and sour cream).

Shiki Four Seasons (££)

The Four Seasons is an authentic Japanese restaurant that specialises in sushi, sashimi and tempura, but more Western dishes like steaks also feature on the menu.

🖂 Zsigmond tér 8, Budapest II
☎ 335 4249

Söröző a Szent Jupáthoz (£)

This highly recommended restaurant serves mainly Hungarian dishes from an extensive menu. The Faust-sized portions are excellently prepared and cooked, and there is a good selection of beers and wines on offer. This place can be heavy on the stomach but light on the wallet. Be prepared to share a table; here you'll find a genial atmosphere and harassed staff.

🖂 Retek utca, Budapest II
☎ 212 1923 ⏱ Lunch, dinner

Széchenyi Restaurant (££)

This restaurant is based at the Ramada Grand Hotel at the northern edge of Margaret Island, and offers a fine view of the park. The speciality is Ramada turkey stew in dill and cucumber sauce, plus a selection of good Hungarian wines and beers.

🖂 Margit-sziget, Budapest XIII
☎ 452 6200 ⏱ Lunch, dinner

Szeged Vendéglő (£)

This is a traditional Hungarian restaurant next to the Gellért Hotel specialising in fish dishes, and also Hungarian and French cuisine. Another feature is live gypsy music and a folk programme.

🖂 Bartók Béla út 1, Budapest XI ☎ 209 1668 ⏱ Lunch, dinner

Tabáni Kakas (£)

This excellent game restaurant with a top reputation is conveniently located behind Castle Hill. A tasty chicken stew with curd-cheese noodles is just one of the specialities.

🖂 Atilla út 27, Budapest I
☎ 375 7165 ⏱ Lunch, dinner

Trombitás (£)

Popular with tour groups, this pub-restaurant serves good Hungarian food, and also features a popular folklore show in the evening.

🖂 Retek utca 12, Budapest II
☎ 212 3154 ⏱ Lunch, dinner

Új Sipos Halászkert (££)

The restaurant, in the picturesque main square of Old Buda, specialises in a wide selection of river fish from Hungarian lakes and rivers, as well as other Hungarian dishes.

🖂 Főtér 6, Budapest III ☎ 250 8156 ⏱ Lunch, dinner

Vadrózsa (£££)

Excellent food is served in a small baroque villa also offering open-air dining in a pleasant garden. Specialities include grilled goose liver and a variety of game dishes, accompanied by fine Hungarian wines. Piano music completes the scene.

🖂 Pentelei Molnár utca 15, Budapest II ☎ 326 5817 ⏱ Lunch, dinner

Valentine Restaurant (£££)

Occupying the gallery of the Várkert Casino, the Valentine serves excellent Hungarian and international cuisine and comes with views of the Danube.

🖂 Ybl Miklós tér, Budapest I
☎ 202 4244 ⏱ Dinner

Pest

Astoria Empire (££)
As the name suggests, this a very plush restaurant set in the impressive Astoria Hotel. Elegant surroundings complement the high standards of Hungarian and international food and wine. Gypsy bands play in the evening.
⊠ Kossuth Lajos utca 19–21, Budapest V ☎ 317 3411
🕔 Lunch, dinner

Bagolyvár (££)
Good, wholesome food served in a convivial atmosphere on the edge of City Park. The restaurant specialises in 'homestyle' Hungarian cooking.
⊠ Állatkerti út 2, Budapest VI
☎ 351 6395 🕔 Lunch, dinner

Belcanto (££)
This restaurant is by the Opera House and its waiters sing from well-known operas. Good international cuisine
⊠ Dalszinház utca 8, Budapest VI ☎ 269 3101 🕔 Lunch, dinner

Bombay Palace (£)
Part of an international chain with a comprehensive menu, the Bombay has a high standard of cooking and presentation in pleasant surroundings.
⊠ Andrássy út 44, Budapest VI
☎ 332 8363 🕔 Lunch, dinner

Café Kör (£)
Traditional Hungarian and European food served in generous portions. Fine salad plates. The Café Kör is located near St Stephen's Basilica.
⊠ Sas utca 17, Budapest V
☎ 311 0053 🕔 Lunch, dinner. Closed Sun

Centrál Kávéház (££)
Old time café refurbished and renovated, it serves breakfast, snacks and meals until late. Located right in the city centre.
⊠ Károlyi Mihály utca 9, Budapest V ☎ 266 2110

Chez Daniel (££)
Here at Chez Daniel the small, select menu of excellent dishes is carefully and affectionately prepared. A good wine and beer list is available. Reservations are necessary.
⊠ Sziv utca 32, Budapest VI
☎ 302 4039 🕔 Lunch, dinner. Closed Sun, Mon early afternoon

Corvinus Restaurant (£££)
The restaurant of the Kempinski Hotel Corvinus, this offers innovative cuisine in a cosy atmosphere. Business lunch served Monday to Friday.
⊠ Erzsébet tér 7–8, Budapest V
☎ 429 3777 🕔 Lunch, dinner. Closed Sun

Cyrano (££)
With its finely designed interior and waiters to match, this is restaurant is a favourite of the Budapest business community. It offers a good menu with a selection of reasonably priced wines. The restaurant prides itself (hence its name) on being a location for the filming of Cyrano de Bergerac.
⊠ Kristóf tér 7–8, Budapest V
☎ 266 3096 🕔 Lunch, dinner

Dionysos (£)
On Pest Quay with an interior like an Hellenic village square, this restaurant is located in attractive surroundings and serves a

A Quiet Table
Many restaurants frequented by visitors have live gypsy bands where the musicians approach the tables to play a song on request, in return for a gratuity. If you don't want to be disturbed during your meal, avoid this type of venue or ask for a table away from the band.

Restaurant Tips

When eating out, be wary of accepting the waiter's offer of the speciality of the house without checking the price. Study the menu for hidden extras such as the price of garnishes and always ask for an itemised bill. Drinks also tend to be pricey in good restaurants. Where service is not included, waiters usually expect a tip of 10–20 per cent.

good choice of excellent dishes.

✉ **Belgrád rakpart 16, Budapest V** ☎ 318 1222
🕒 **Lunch, dinner**

Fatál (£)

Fatál, a traditional restaurant, offers wholesome, homestyle Hungarian dishes, with salads and vegetarian entrées served on wooden plates. The portions are generous, as is the welcome. Payment by cash only.

✉ **Váci utca 67 (entrance on Pintér utca), Budapest V**
☎ 266 2607 🕒 **Lunch, dinner**

La Fontaine (££)

This bistro-style restaurant is conveniently located in the heart of the town. It serves modestly priced typical French dishes, and has a full range of wines, beers and spirits.

✉ **Mérleg utca 10, Pest V,** ☎ 317 3715 🕒 **Lunch, dinner**

Gandhi (£)

The Gandhi, a vegetarian restaurant, has new dishes daily with excellent French salads. Soups and teas from purified water and wheat beer are also available. There is a smokeless, candlelit interior with pleasant, soothing music. Take-out available.

✉ **Vigyázó Ferenc út 4, Budapest V** ☎ 269 1625
🕒 **Lunch, dinner**

Gundel (£££)

Hungary's most famous restaurant (Britain's Queen Elizabeth II ate here, hence the prices), situated on the edge of City Park by the Zoological Gardens. The Gundel has been restored to

its *fin-de-siècle* splendour, and smart dress is required. Brunch is served on Sunday.

✉ **Állatkerti út 3, Budapest XIV**
☎ 321 3550 🕒 **Lunch, dinner**

Iguana Bar & Grill (££)

Frequented by home-sick American expatriates, the Iguana serves excellent Mexican food and margaritas in a lively Hungarian and international atmosphere.

✉ **Zoltán utca 16, Budapest V**
☎ 331 4352 🕒 **Lunch, dinner**

Kispesti Halásztanya (££)

Excellent fish dishes are served in a country-inn interior, with gypsy music in the evening. Payment by cash only.

✉ **Városhaz tér 6, Budapest XIX** ☎ 282 9873 🕒 **Lunch, dinner**

Lou Lou (££)

This French restaurant with Hungarian appeal serves fresh vegetables even in winter, and offers a good choice of wines, beers and spirits.

✉ **Vigyázó F. utca 4, Budapest V** ☎ 312 4505 🕒 **Lunch, dinner. Closed Sun**

Művészinas (££)

This stylish bistro offers fine and varied food, vintage Hungarian wines and good beers in a pleasant location with air-conditioning.

✉ **Bajcsy-Zsilinszky út 9, Budapest VI** ☎ 268 1439
🕒 **Lunch, dinner**

Múzeum Kávéház (££)

Set in a beautiful 19th-century coffee house next to the National Museum, with original Karoly Lot's frescoes inside, you may find your appetite more than satisfied by the aesthetics of this place. Piano music is a feature in the evening.

✉ **Múzeum körút 12, Budapest III** ☎ **267 0375** 🕐 **Lunch, dinner. Closed Sun**

Okay Italia (£)

Run by Italians, the pizzas and fresh pasta here are exquisite, and served in a friendly, vibrant atmosphere. But be prepared to have a drink at the bar while you wait. Accepts cash only.

✉ **Szent István körút 20, Budapest XIII** ☎ **332 6960** 🕐 **Lunch, dinner**

Old Timer Restaurant (£££)

Situated in the luxury Regency Hyatt Hotel, this restaurant offers excellent food and wines, and splendid views of the Danube, but at a price.

✉ **Roosevelt tér 2, Budapest V** ☎ **266 1234** 🕐 **Lunch, dinner**

Resti (£)

You cannot get nearer the city centre, though you may still not notice this place with communist nostalgia décor of red stars and agitprop posters. It serves Hungarian dishes at very reasonable prices.

✉ **Deák Ferenc utca 2, Budapest V** ☎ **266 6210** 🕐 **Lunch, dinner**

Robinson (££)

The Robinson is romantically located on the lake by Heroes' Square, a feature reflected in the prices. The menu is not extensive, but don't miss 'Robinson Palacsinta,' a crêpe filled with vanilla cream and fresh-fruit salad. Business lunches served.

✉ **Városliget Lake, Budapest XIV** ☎ **422 0222** 🕐 **Lunch, dinner**

Sir Lancelot (£)

Enormous portions are served on wooden plates by waiters in period costume. Live Renaissance music in the evenings.

✉ **Podmaniczky utca 14, Budapest V** ☎ **302 4456** 🕐 **Lunch, dinner**

Soul Café (£)

On a street bustling with recently opened restaurants and bars. It has a good atmosphere and tasty Mediterranean cuisine.

✉ **Ráday utca 11–13, Budapest IX** ☎ **217 6986** 🕐 **Lunch, dinner**

Via Luna (£)

The restaurant is located behind the Natinal Bank and has an extensive Italian menu with a large choice of salads. Lively atmosphere.

✉ **Nagysándor utca 1, Budapest V** ☎ **312 8058** 🕐 **Lunch, dinner**

Vista Café (£)

A café and restaurant, the Vista also offers internet access and tourist information. Contemporary, tasty international cuisine. There is live jazz music at weekends.

✉ **Paulay Ede utca 7, Budapest VII** ☎ **268 0888** 🕐 **Lunch, dinner**

Vörös és Fehér (££)

The name, Red and White, is an appropriate one for the restaurant of the Budapest Wine Society. Excellent wines by the glass, too.

✉ **Andrássy út 41, Budapest VI** ☎ **413 1545** 🕐 **Lunch, dinner**

Café Society

Cafés held a unique place in Budapest life from the mid-19th century, when they were fashionable meeting places among the city's intellectual, artistic and social circles. They opened round the clock and became breeding grounds for a range of activities: one was the editorial office of the first Central European cinema weekly, inspiring the famous film producer Sir Alexander Korda. The vibrant café society dwindled after World War II, but a few places still offer glimpses into the past.

Buda

Price bands below refer to approximate cost per room, per night:

£ = budget
(up to 17,500 HUF)
££ = moderate
(17,000–44,500 HUF)
£££ = expensive
(44,500–56,000 HUF)

Ábel Guest House (£)
This small but comfortable place, in a quiet area just south west of the Citadel, has 10 rooms, all with bathroom and phones.
✉ Ábel Jenő utca 9, Budapest XI ☎ 209 2537; fax 209 2538

Aquincum Corinthia (££)
Situated on the Buda river front, with some interesting architectural sites near by, this takes its Roman name from the first sizeable settlement in the region. This is a five-star hotel in a good location, and some of its 312 rooms offer views across to Margaret Island.
✉ Árpád fejedelem útja, 94, Budapest III ☎ 436 4100/436 4700

Buda Center Hotel (££)
With 34 rooms and three family apartments, this is conveniently situated a few minutes from the city centre at the foot of Castle Hill.
✉ Csalogány út 23, Budapest II ☎ 201 6333; fax 201 7843

Carlton Hotel (££)
This spacious hotel with 95 rooms and good facilities is situated at the bottom of Castle Hill. But there are no memorable views.
✉ Apor Péter utca 3, Budapest I ☎ 224 0999; fax 224 0990 📠 19

Danubius Grand Hotel (£££)
A four-star establishment with 164 rooms, this old spa hotel shares a beautiful setting with the Danubius Thermal Hotel on Margaret Island in the middle of the Danube.
✉ Margit-sziget, Budapest XIII ☎ 452 6200

Danubius Hotel Gellért (££)
This traditional *fin-de-siècle* spa hotel with a magnificent pool has a mosaic floor and glass ceiling. A comfortable, four-star hotel with 239 rooms,it has a blissful indifference to the demands of modern life, and features a splendid restaurant with views of the Danube.
✉ Szent Gellért tér 1, Budapest XI, ☎ 385 2200

Danubius Thermal Hotel Margit-sziget (£££)
This modern spa hotel is much less elegant than the Danubius Grand (▶ pevious column) but the location on Margaret Island is very attractive, as is its four-star rating. There are 206 rooms.
✉ Margit-sziget, Budapest XI11 ☎ 452 6200

Dunapart (££)
Anchored at the Buda embankment is this floating 32-room hotel in a converted steamer. Prices depend on whether your room has a view of the Parliament building or the noisy, car-strewn embankment. The Dunapart also has a reasonably good restaurant.
✉ Szilágyi Dezső tér, Budapest I ☎ 355 9001

Hilton Hotel (£££)
A pearl in the Hilton chain, this modern 323-room hotel in the Castle District blends tastefully with its picturesque surroundings and, naturally, offers high standards all round.
✉ Hess András tér 1–3, Budapest I ☎ 488 6600

Hotel Budapest (£££)
A large, multi–storey modern hotel within walking distance

of Castle Hill, this is a business and conference-orientated hotel, but offers fine views of Buda.

📧 **Szilágyi Erzsébet fasor 47, Budapest I** ☎ **488 8900; fax 488 9808**

Hotel Citadella (£)

As its name suggests, this small and basic 15-room hotel is well located on near the Citadel on top of Gellert Hill. Facilities include a restaurant and brasserie, and also a private parking area.

📧 **Citadella sétány, Budapest XI** ☎ **466 5794; fax 486 0505**

Kulturinnov (££)

This is modest, dormitory-type rooms but is comfortable and reasonably priced. Its attraction – besides being not too expensive – is that it is only 200m from Matthias Church in the beautiful Castle District. Some parts grand, some shabby.

📧 **Szentháromság tér 6, Budapest I** ☎ **355 0122; fax 375 3367** 🚌 **Bus 16, Várbusz**

Mercure Buda (££)

This is located between the Southern (Déli) Railway Station and beautiful Blood Field, or Vérmezo, which commemorates the executions of Jacobins in 1795. One side has a panoramic view of Castle Hill. The hotel is not especially pleasing to look at but the 399 rooms offer good views.

📧 **Krisztina körút 41–43, Budapest I** ☎ **488 8100**

Novotel Budapest Centrum (££)

This hotel stands beside the Budapest Convention Centre on the road leading to Elizabeth Bridge. It has 324 comfortable rooms and good facilities, but it is let down by its location.

📧 **Alkotás utca 63–67, Budapest XII** ☎ **372 5700**

Orion Hotel (££)

At the foot of Castle Hill, this hotel has 31-rooms with air-conditioning, TVs and phones. There is also an international restaurant.

📧 **Döbrentei utca 13, Budapest I** ☎ **356 8583; fax 375 5418**

Panoráma (££)

The hotel is situated by the terminus of the cogwheel railway (Fogaskerekű Vasút) on top of Szabadság-hegy; insist on a booking in the main building if you want a panoramic view.

📧 **Rege utca 21, Budapest XII** ☎ **395 6121**

Parkhotel Flamenco (£££)

This is a well-located, large and modern hotel, just south of Gellért Hill a few minutes from the business and shopping areas. With 348 rooms, including 10 suites, it offers a wide range of facilities: restaurant and numerous bars, live music, car rental, a business centre and full leisure facilities.

📧 **Tas vezér utca 7, Budapest XI** ☎ **372 2000; fax 365 8007**

Victoria (££)

Situated on the Buda riverbank, this comfortable 27-room hotel with full facilities overlooks the old Chain Bridge and is within easy reach of many of the major sights.

📧 **Bem rakpart 11, Budapest I** ☎ **457 8080; fax 457 8088** 🚌 **Bus 16, tram 19**

Finding a Room

Budapest has a wide range of accommodation, including everything from luxury hotels to private rooms. The city has almost 100 hotels and nearly 2,000 other types of accommodation to choose from, so you should find something to suit your taste and budget. The Tourist Office issues two helpful catalogues: one of hotels, pensions (*panzió*) and hostels; the other listing campsites. Contact Tourinform ☎ 117 9800.

Pest

Youth Hostels
Young people and students travelling to Budapest are well catered for by youth hostels. The official Hostelling International office at Keleti (Eastern) Station has details of a large selection of centrally located hostels in the city, offering a range of facilities and services.

Astoria (££)
Featuring sumptuous splendour with a *fin-de-siècle* atmosphere, some have likened the Astoria to a gentlemen's club – an ambiguous tribute. There is nothing remotely geriatric about this pleasant three-star hotel with 130 rooms, but it is very relaxing and unhurried.

✉ **Kossuth Lajos utca 19–21, Budapest V** ☎ **317 3411**

City Panzió Pilvax (£)
The hotel opens to a pedestrian street in the city centre. The comfortable rooms all offer en suite facilities.

✉ **Pilvax köz 1–3, Budapest V** ☎ **266 7660**

Fortuna (£)
A boat hotel on the Danube across from Margaret Island. Cabins are comfortable although they are naturally smaller than average hotel rooms.

✉ **Szent István Park, alsó rakpart (lower embankment of the Danube), Budapest XIII** ☎ **288 8100**

Erzsébet (££)
A comfortable, three-star establishment with 123 air-conditioned rooms, the Erzsébet is ideally situated at the heart of town close to the popular shopping street of Váci utca and the city's business centre. Facilities at the hotel include a restaurant, bar and pub, car rental and a business centre.

✉ **Károlyi Mihály utca 11–15, Budapest V** ☎ **328 5700; fax: 328 5763**

Grand Hotel Hungaria (££)
Located just ten minutes' walk from the inner city, the four-star Hungaria is the largest hotel in Hungary. It serves a good range of excellent food in the Fiaker Söröző, or Beer Hall, and some of the 511 rooms have views of the impressive Keleti (Eastern) Railway Station.

✉ **Rákóczi út 90, Budapest VII** ☎ **478 1100**

Ibis Centrum (££)
Right in the city centre and close to the shopping and business areas the hotel has 126 rooms which benefit from soundproofed windows. It has a garage and a roof garden. There are rooms for guests with disabilities and non-smokers.

✉ **Ráday utca 6, Budapest IX** ☎ **215 8585**

K + K Hotel Opera (££)
This hotel was purpose-built for music lovers and is situated just 50m from the Opera House. Guests in any of the 205 rooms are treated to immaculate service and the hotel also offers good a good range of leisure facilities.

✉ **Révay útca 24, Budapest VI** ☎ **269 0222; fax 269 0230**

Kempinski Hotel Corvinus (£££)
This striking, post-modern hotel boasts three elegant façades and one plain one. It has 368 rooms/suites including two luxurious presidential apartments, and also caters for guests with disabilities.

✉ **Erzsébet tér 7–8, Budapest V** ☎ **429 3777**

Liget Hotel (££)
The Liget is a reasonably

priced three-star, 160-room hotel in a prime city-centre location overlooking both the impressive Fine Arts Museum (► 25) and the Zoo in City Park.

✉ **Dózsa György út 106, Budapest VI** ☎ **269 5300**

Mercure Korona (££)

Occupying a downtown prime site on noisy Kálvin tér, this 433-room hotel provides excellent access to all the sights, and is just a three-minute walk from the river.

✉ **Kecskeméti utca 14, Budapest V** ☎ **317 4111**

Mercure Metropol (£)

This 100-room hotel in a busy downtown setting has basic facilities but is reasonably comfortable.

✉ **Rákóczi út 58, Budapest VII** ☎ **462 8100**

Mercure Nemzeti (££)

Traditional splendour of the Grand Boulevard days is on offer here with 76 rooms, suites and a conference room. However, the hotel is built over an underground station, Blaha Lujza tér.

✉ **József körút 4, Budapest VIII** ☎ **477 2000**

Le Meridien Budapest (£££)

Located in an elegant building, which has been declared an historic monument, this luxurious hotel has 218 rooms decorated with period furniture and chandeliers. A beautiful atrium, with a stained-glass dome, is the setting for Le Bourbon restaurant. This city centre hotel is close to the main business and shopping

districts and the main sights, including the Danube.

✉ **Erzsébet tér 9–10, Budapest V** ☎ **267 4545**

Radio Inn (£)

Spacious apartments in the quiet leafy diplomaic district near the city centre, with good public transport.

✉ **Benczur utca 19, Budapest VI** ☎ **342 8347**

Radisson SAS Béke (££)

The Radisson is a modernised 246-room hotel on the city's main thoroughfare, the Grand Boulevard. Good eating can be had in the Shakespeare Restaurant, with a pleasant café serving excellent sweets and espresso.

✉ **Teréz körút 43, Budapest VI** ☎ **301 1600**

Regency Budapest Hyatt (£££)

This international hotel and conference centre with 355 rooms and 28 apartments is suave, efficient, comfortable and has all the modern conveniences of a top-class hotel. You can order an official replica of any of the paintings in the National Gallery. They have it painted for you and it comes issued with a certificate as well.

✉ **Roosevelt tér 2, Budapest V** ☎ **266 1234**

Taverna (££)

Located on Budapest's fashionable shopping street, the Taverna is a very functional concrete-and-glass four-star hotel – part of an entertainment complex – with 196 rooms and all the ususal modern facilities.

✉ **Váci utca 20, Budapest V** ☎ **485 3100**

Central Locations

A great number of Budapest's hotels are concentrated on the Pest side of the Danube, close to many of the major sights. The Hotel Association of Hungary publishes a useful booklet detailing its member hotels, from five-star establishments to pensions, in the Budapest region.

Outside Budapest

Prices (Outside Budapest)
Accommodation is generally cheaper outside Budapest. The price bands below represent the approximate cost (excluding a tourist tax of 0.3 per cent) of a double room with private facilities, per night.

£ = budget
(up to 12,000 HUF)
££ = moderate
(12,000–19,000 HUF)
£££ = expensive (over 19,000 HUF)

Balatonfüred
Annabella Hotel £££
Caters for 'healthy' holidays on the shores of Lake Balaton. Family orientated with a populist appeal.
✉ 8230 Deák Ferenc utca 25, Balatonfüred ☎ (87) 342 222; fax (87) 343 084

Marina (££)
Offering watersports, beaches and excellent facilities, this popular hotel has 350 rooms.
✉ Széchenyi utca 26 ☎ (87) 343 644

Debrecen
Cívis (£££)
One of the finest hotels in Debrecen, set in a pleasant square. It offers a wide variety of facilities, including (if you need it) dental treatment.
✉ Kálvin tér 4 ☎ (52) 410 111

Debrecen (£)
A basic hotel with few facilities but clean, well-maintained and hospitable.
✉ Petőfi tér 9 ☎ (52) 316 550

Eger
Eger Hotel & Park Hotel (£££)
Handsome, modern, questionably stylish hotel offering a variety of entertainments, from Bowling Beerhouse to wine tasting in the Valley of Beautiful Women,
✉ 3300 Szálloda ut 1–3, Eger ☎ (36) 413 233; fax (36) 413 114

Hotel Korona (£££)
In a quiet spot, this boasts a 200-year-old wine cellar, a conference room and a terrace restaurant.
✉ 3300 Tünderpárt ut 5, Eger ☎ (36) 313 670; fax (36) 310 261

Minaret (££)
Close to the famous Turkish Minaret, it offers standard facilities but benefits from its central location.
✉ Knézich Károly utca 4 ☎ (36) 410 020

Panoráma Panzió (£)
A pension with good facilities, including a sauna and, as the name suggests, excellent views of this beautiful town. Ask for a room with a view.
✉ Joo János utca 9 ☎ (36) 420 531

Esztergom
Beta Hotel Esztergom (££)
One of the principal hotels in this fascinating old town, offering all modern facilities for its 36 rooms. Conveniently situated for all the main attractions and sights.
✉ Prímás-sziget, Nagy-Duna sétány ☎ (33) 412 555

Judit Panzio (£)
Basic, but ideal for a cheap stay with no frills. Emphasises family hospitality. Permits dogs, if you have brought yours.
✉ 2500 Mattyasovszky ut 19, Esztergom ☎ (33) 411 372

Platán Panzio (£)
Cheap, clean, comfortable with ample hospitality. Few mod cons but it does boast a conference room!
✉ 2500 Kis–Duna sétány 11, Esztergom ☎ fax (33) 411 355

Szent Kristóf Panzió (£)
One of the top pensions in Esztergom, it is set in garden surrounds with a coffee lounge and beer parlour.
✉ Dobazi Mihály utca 11 ☎ (33) 416 255

Győr

Kiskút–Liget Motel & Camping (£)
Excellent facilities for both the sporty and the sloth, with comfortable well-furnished rooms and camping grounds.
✉ 9027 Kiskúti út 41/A, Győr
☎ /fax (96) 517 126

Klastrom (££)
In an attractive setting in the beautiful old town of Győr, this hotel offers good facilities, including a sauna, solarium and air-conditioned rooms.
✉ Zechmeister utca 1
☎ (96) 516 910

Pannon-Flax (£)
Basic but comfortable, this is good value for money if you are looking for modest 'no-frills' hotel accommodation. Centrally located and with facilities for visitors with disabilities.
✉ Kandó Kálmán utca 1
☎ (96) 315 766

Héviz

Lotusz Hotel (£)
Clean, accommodating but basic. It does however boast private parking, its only luxury apparently.
✉ 8380 Honved ut 2, Heviz
☎ (83) 343 325

Hollókő

Panoráma Panzió & Camping (£)
If you are camping this is an ideal location for visiting Hollókő, one of Hungary's most attractive and historic villages. The pension itself has a wine bar, restaurant and facilities for those with disabilities.
✉ Orgona utca 31
☎ (32) 379 048

Kecskemét

Aranyhomok (££)
Centrally located in the attractive old town of Kecskemét, approximately 60km southeast of Budapest, this pleasant hotel offers fine service and a full range of facilities.
✉ Kossuth tér 3 ☎ (76) 486286

Szentendre

Duna Club (££)
One of the best hotels in Szentendre on the Danube Bend, the Duna Club offers a beach for sunbathing and a swimming pool among its many facilities.
✉ Duna korzó 5 ☎ (26) 314 102

Panzió No 100 (£)
Since various types of fish are a speciality in Hungarian cuisine, perhaps some angling (boats provided) at this comfortable pension might be just the thing. Horse trekking is also one of the activities available.
✉ Ady Endre út 100 ☎ (26) 310 373

Bükkös Panzió (£)
Comfortable, pleasantly situated pension offering hotel amenities at pension rates.
✉ 2000 Bükkös-part 16, Szentendre ☎ (26) 312 021; fax 310 722

Danubius Hotel (££)
Standard Hungarian chain hotel with all the usual facilities. Comfortable, adequate, and set in pleasant surroundings. Camping and restaurant on adjacent Pap Island.
✉ 2000 Ady Endre út 28, Szentendre ☎ /fax (26) 312 511

Local Traditions
The Magyar language is unfamiliar enough to Western ears, but, if you are staying outside Budapest, especially in the north of Hungary, you may also hear a dialect known as Palóc. Villages in this region, for example Hollókő, revel in their folk traditions and you will be treated to some of the most colourful costumes in the country, especially on Sunday and during Easter celebrations.

Antiques & Art

Where to Shop
If you do not have much time, it is best to go shopping in the Inner City, though it may be expensive (Váci utca, Petőfi Sándor utca, Régiposta utca, Haris köz, Párizsi utca, Kigyó utca). If you have more time, shop along Kossuth Lajos utca, Rákóczi út, Károly körút, Múzeum körút, Szent István körút, Erzsébet Körút and József körút.

Antik Bazár
True to its name, it has a wonderful array of antiques but specialises in antique linens, dresses, shawls, dolls and jewellery. A cosy place.
⊠ **Váci utca 67, Budapest V**
☎ **418 1478**

Antik Diszkont
A cash only shop specialising in furniture and chandeliers in a variety of styles. Not really for small-item hunters.
⊠ **Falk Miksa utca 22, Budapest V** ☎ **302 3077**

Arten Gallery
A stimulating and well-exhibited selection of contemporary Hungarian artists such as Arnold Gross.
⊠ **Váci utca 25, Budapest V**
☎ **266 3127**

BÁV
Bizományi Árúhaz Vállalat (BÁV), the state-owned chain offers one of the best chances to pick up a bargain. The outlets sell paintings, jewellery, carpets, porcelain, rugs and furnishings. Among the many branches is the one at:
⊠ **Bécsi utca 1–3, Budapest V**
☎ **318 3381**

Csók István Gallery
Certainly one of the best galleries if you want to buy contemporary Hungarian art.
⊠ **Váci utca 25, Budapest V**
☎ **318 5826**

Dovin Gallery
Work by the celebrated Hungarian artist Peter Gemes is exhibited for sale here.
⊠ **Galamb utca 6, Budapest V**
☎ **318 3673**

Forgács
A superb choice of quality books, prints and antiques in very pleasant surroundings.
⊠ **Kempinski Hotel Corvinus, Erzsébet tér 7–8, Budapest V**
☎ **266 1000**

Galléria Kieselbach
There is a continually changing stock of paintings on display here, including avante-garde Hungarian works, Old Masters and furniture.
⊠ **Szent István körút 5, Budapest V** ☎ **269 3148**

Horterius
Mainly specialising in engravings and antiques, but has some books to browse through.
⊠ **Múzeum körút 35, Budapest V** ☎ **317 3270**

Koller
Works by sculptors and painters such as Imre Varga. Well worth a visit if only to browse the beautiful exhibits.
⊠ **Táncsics Mihály út 5, Budapest 1** ☎ **356 9208**

Nagyházi Galéria
The gallery offers an extensive choice of furniture, paintings, lamps and *objet d'art*.
⊠ **Balaton utca 8, Budapest V**
☎ **331 9908**

Polgár
Private dealer with a superb collection of furniture, carved ivory and much more.
⊠ **Kossuth Lajos utca 3, Budapest V** ☎ **318 6954**

Qualitás
Veritable emporium of paintings, furniture, porcelain and objets d'art.
⊠ **Falk Miksa utca 32, Budapest V** ☎ **311 8471**

Books & Fashion

Books

Bestsellers
Wide range of fiction and non-fiction, magazines, guides, dictionaries. Ordering service available. The best English-language bookshop.
 Október 6 út 11, Budapest V
☎ 312 1295

Fókusz
Occupying two large floors, this is the biggest bookshop in Hungary.
✉ Rákótzi út 14, Budapest VII

Helikon
Large, lavishly decorated two-level bookshop with a comprehensive selection of Hungarian and foreign books and a small café in the basement.
✉ Bajcsy-Zsilinszky út 37, corner Hajós utca, Budapest VI

Központi Antikvárium
The Central Antiquarian Bookshop, established in 1881, with a huge selection of maps and foreign books.
✉ Múzeum körút 13–15, Budapest V ☎ 317 3781

Nyugat Antikvárium
Shelves of rare foreign-language books, prints and maps that can keep you browsing for hours.
✉ Bajcsy-Zsilinszky út 34, Budapest V ☎ 311 9023
 Arany János utca

Osiris Könyvesház
Egghead bookshop for eggheads but definitely well worth a visit if only for the atmosphere. Just go in, sit down and read anything that takes your fancy. Studiously informal.
✉ Veres Pálné utca 4–6, Budapest V ☎ 318 2516

Párisi Udvar Bookshop
Stocked with guidebooks, maps, books on Hungary, picture albums in a variety of languages, plus CDs, diaries and folk-art objects.
✉ Petőfi Sándor utca 2, Budapest V ☎ 235 0379

Fashion

Carum Carvi Fashion House
If you fancy a made-to-measure suit or just one off the peg this shop, for men and women, is well worth a visit.
✉ Pest V, Kossuth Lajos utca 17 🕐 Mon–Fri 10–6, Sat 10–1

Classic Line
Famous designer clothes for women and men. An elegant and exclusive shop offering the latest international fashions.
✉ Andrássy út 28, Budapest VI ☎ 331 2837 🕐 Mon–Fri 11–7, Sat 10–2

Gafarino
Smart, trendy men's shop that claims unbeatable prices.
✉ Pest V1, Bajcsy–Zsillinszky ut 45 ☎ 302 5432 🕐 Mon–Fri 10–6, Sat 10–2

Imagine Moda
Stylish clothing and accessories for men and women from the Cinque line.
✉ Pest V, Vitkovits Mihály utca 3–5 🕐 Mon–Fri 11–7, Sat 11–4

Versace
As the name implies, smart, stylish clothing from the big names for men and women.
✉ Pest V, Universum Centrum, Vaci utca 31–33 ☎ 267 2665. 🕐 Mon–Fri 10–7, Sat 10–3

Budapest Card
You may find it convenient to buy the Budapest Card when out and about. Valid for three days, it offers free travel on public transport, visits to museums, 50 per cent reduction on guided tours and varying discounts at a number of places, from baths to shops, restaurants to the airport minibus. On sale at tourist information bureaux, hotels, travel agencies, museums and major BKV ticket offices, it costs 2,900 HUF for adults and 2,000 HUF for children under 14.

Gifts, Jewellery
& Music

Opening Times
Most shops are open from 10 to 6 Monday to Friday and 9 to 1 Saturday with grocery stores and supermarkets open from 8AM.

China & Glass

Herend Porcelain
A wide selection of Hungary's most famous porcelain (the factory was established in 1826), including table sets, individual pieces, decorative items, lamps and Swarovski crystal figurines can be bought at two elegant shops in the city.
✉ József Nádor tér 11 ☎ 317 2622 ✉ Kígyó utca 3 ☎ 318 3439

Herendi Majolika
Herend 'village pottery' and Ajika crystal ranging from table services to individual pieces.
✉ Bem rakpart, Budapest I ☎ 356 7899 🕐 Tue–Fri–5, Sat 9–12

Hollóháza
Beautiful, high-quality northeast Hungarian pottery which began manufacturing porcelain in 1954.
✉ Marriot Hotel Pergola, Apáczai Csere János utca, Budapest V ☎ 266 7000

Opal Art
Excellent shop selling glassware in the Castle District. Specialises in popular contemporaray and art nouveau designs
✉ Fortuna Passage, Hess András tér, Budapest V ☎ 405 5784 🕐 Daily10–5

Zsolnay
Here you can find original Zsolnay porcelain from the town of Pecs, including table services, vases and individual pieces.
✉ Kígyó utca 4, Budapest V ☎ 318 3712 🕐 Mon–Fri 10–6, Sat 10–1

Leather Goods

La Boutique
Designer Italian shoes, bags and fine accessories. The best in Budapest.
✉ Andrássy út 16, Budapest VI ☎ 302 5646

Vass
Pay a visit to this traditonal shoemaker for a pair of hand-made leather shoes or just ready to wear.
✉ Haris köz 2, Budapest V ☎ 318 2375

Jewellery

Pless & Fox
Here you can find all kinds of jewellery and rare metals. The shop specialises in diamonds but do not expect a bargain.
✉ Szent István körút 18, Budapest XIII ☎ 340 4333

Music

Ferenc Liszt Zeneubolt
A comprehensive selection of Cds, cassettes, records is available here.
✉ Pest V1, Andrássy út 45 🕐 Mon–Fri 10–6, Sat 10–1

Rózsavölgyi
This is an olld established music shop specialising in classical music and sheet music. Also folk and rock sections.
✉ Pest V, Szervita tér 5, tel. 318 3500 🕐 Mon–Fri 10–6, Sat 10–2

Zoltán Kodály Music Shop
Cds, records, cassettes, old and new sheet music, some first editions.
✉ Pest V Múzeum körút 21 ☎ 317 3247 🕐 Mon–Fri 10–6, Sat 10–3

Food & Drink/ Speciality Shops

Food & Drink

Ági Gyümölcs Greengrocers
This is a small corner shop reputedly offering the freshest and best-quality produce in the area. Family photographs adorn the wall, interspersed with motorcyle advertisements.
✉ Tátra utca 20, Budapest XIII

Bakator Wine Store
A typical Hungarian wine shop selling an excellent range of wines at very reasonable prices.
✉ V1 Jókai ter 7, off Andrássy ut ☎ 353 4849

La Boutique des Vins
This shop offers an excellent selection of Hungarian and international wines, expert advice is also on hand.
✉ V, Jozsef Attila utca 12 ☎ 117 5919

Budapest Bortársaság (Wine Society)
A fine selection of over 100 wines from Hungarian vintners, with free tasting on Saturdays.
✉ Batthyány tér 59, Budapest I ☎ 212 2569

Demi John
Owned by the famous Interconsult Winery Neszmely, this outlet specialises in its own outstanding wines.
✉ V, Cukor utca 4 ☎ 326 4984

Dóczy Delicatessen
Here you'll find an excellent range of Hungarian and international delicacies, wines and liqueurs.
✉ Országház utca 16, Budapest I ☎ 212 3761

Exclusive Wines
Exclusive in tone it may be, but it stocks a very inclusive selection of fine wines.
✉ Régiposta utca 7–9, Budapest V ☎ 118 7972

The House of Hungarian Wines
The richest selection of Hungarian wines to buy and taste in a real cellar divided into wine growing regions of Hungary. Located opposite the Hilton Hotel in the Castle district.
✉ Szentháromság tér 6, Budapest I ☎ 212 1031

Wine City
Although the name sounds like supermarket shopping, don't be deceived – the choice of wines here is excellent.
✉ V, Párisi utca 1 ☎ 318 2683

Speciality Shops

Dénes Vándorffy
An extraordinary range of buttons exclusively for women.
✉ Váci utca 75, Budapest V

Fleisher Shirts
Almost unchanged since it opened in the 1920s, Fleisher's is a bespoke tailor.
✉ Corner of Paulay Ede utca and Nagymező utca, Budapest VI

Tobacconist
A splendidly run-down, shabby little shop selling everything under the sun – from shoelaces to magnifying glasses fastened to pens.
✉ Márvány utca 24/b, Budapest XII

Credit Cards
While most credit cards are accepted in Budapest, never take it for granted. Always carry sufficient cash with you.

Children's Budapest

Plenty to Do

Children are generally well catered for in Budapest. Besides some interesting museums, like the Transport and Stamp museums, there's just about everything to suit the most fastidious taste, from hi-tech entertainment like the Planetarium's Laser Theatre to Magic City, to zoos, funfairs and railways. Also, children under 14 are eligible for reductions on transport and admission fees to several museums and other venues.

Caves

Budavári Labirintus (Budavár Labyrinth)

This extensive system of connecting caves includes various exhibitions, projections and cave art.

✉ Úri utca 9, Budapest I ☎ 212 0207

Castle Cave

In the Castle District is a further section of the labyrinth, consisting of cavity-turned cellars and man-made deep cellars. During the 40-minute guided tour you can see wells, former storerooms and remains of baths and combat stations used by the Germans in World War II.

✉ Corner of Országház utca and Dárda utca, Budapest I
☎ 214 312 ⏰ 10–6 Tue–Sun
🚌 16 Várbusz

Entertainment

Állatkert/Állat-és Növénykert (Municipal Zoological and Botanical Gardens)

One of the oldest zoos in the world, housing an inordinate number of animals, plus some 1,500 plant species.

✉ Állatkerti Körút 6–12, Budapest XIV ☎ 343 6075
⏰ May–Aug, daily 9–7; Sep–Apr, daily 9–5
🚇 Széchenyi fürdo 🚌 4

Fővárosi Nagycirkusz (Municipal Circus)

World-famous Hungarian trapeze artists, plus clowns and tamed animals.

✉ Állatkerti Körút 12, Budapest XIV
⏰ Performances: Mon, Thu, Fri 3PM; Sat 10, 3, 7; Sun 10, 3
🚇 Széchenyi fürdo 🚌 72

Magic City

Based at the Western Village in the Pólus Center (the biggest shopping centre in Central Europe) is this entertainment complex offering a bowling alley, slot machines, ice rink, restaurants and cinemas.

✉ Szentmihályi út 131, Budapest XV ⏰ Mon–Fri 9–7, Sat 9–5, Sun 9–3 🚌 73, 130; Polus shuttle bus from Nyugati and Keleti railway stations

Vidámpark (Amusement Park)

Located in the City Park, the funfair includes a Ferris wheel, roller coaster, shooting gallery, merry-go-round and dodgem cars. The 19th century carousel has recently been reopened after restoration.

✉ Állatkeri Körút 14–16, Budapest XIV ⏰ Apr–Sep, daily 10–8; Oct-Mar, daily 10–6
🚇 Széchenyi fürdó 🚌 72

Museums and Scientific Discovery

Bélyeg Múzuem (Stamp Museum)

More stamps than you could possibly hope to count from all over the world, including Hungarian first editions.

✉ Hársfa út 47, Budapest VII ☎ 341 5526 ⏰ Apr–Oct, Tue–Sun 10–6; Nov–Mar, Tue–Sun 10–4 🚇 4, 6; Trolley 74

Hadtörténeti Múzeum (Museum of War History)

This is will appeal perhaps more to dads and sons. Several exhibitions, with 100,000 weapons, uniforms, medals and flags on display.

⊠ Tóth Árpád Sétány 40, Budapest I ⏲ Apr–Sep Tue–Sun 10–6; Oct–Mar, Tue–Sun 10–4 🚌 16, Várbusz

Hungarian Natural History Museum

Through the history of the Carpathian Basin the exhibition traces Man's development, from the earliest times to the emergence of civilised society.

⊠ Ludovika tér 2, Budapest VIII ☎ 333 0655 ⏲ Wed–Mon 10–6 Ⓜ Klinikák

Közlekdési Múzeum (Transport Museum)

The museum is for the enthusiast of cars, trains, and railways (➤ 65).

Csodák Palotája: Interaktív Tudományos Játszóház (Palace of Wonders: Interactive Scientific Playhouse)

Behind this extensive name is Central Europe's first interactive, scientific playhouse, with more than 100 spectacular, hands-on scientific games and experiments.

⊠ Váci út 19, Budapest XIII ☎ 350 6131 ⏲ Sep–Jun Tue–Fri, 9–5, Sat–Sun 10–6. Closed Jul–Aug Ⓜ Lehel tér.

Planetárium

The largest Hungarian institution of public education on astronomy and space exploration. Includes the Laser Theatre, an awesome display of light effects and music.

⊠ Népliget, Budapest X ⏲ Tue–Sun 9–4; Laser Theatre shows at 7PM Ⓜ Népliget

Uránia Csillagvizsgátó (Urania Observatory)

If the sky is clear, this is the place to see the stars over Hungary.

⊠ Sánc ucta 3/B, Budapest I ⏲ In clear weather: Mon–Fri 6–10 🚌 27

Rides

Gyermek Vasút (Children's Railway)

Narrow-guage railway running along an 11.1km route and supervised (apart from the engineer) by uniformed local children. The train calls at János Hill, the city's highest point.

⊠ Terminus-Hűvösvölgy, Budapest II ⏲ 15 Mar–23 Oct, Mon–Fri 10–6, Sat–Sun 9:45–6:15; 24 Oct–14 Mar, Mon–Fri 10–4, Sat–Sun 10–6 🚋 Tram 56

Libegő (Chairlift)

Something like a ski-lift with chairs hanging from a haulage chain, the 15-minute journey between Zugliget and János Hill offers unforgettable views of Budapest.

⊠ Zugligeti út 93, Budapest ⏲ 16 May–15 Sep, daily 9–5; 16 Sep–15 May, daily 9:30–4 Closed Mon of every even-numbered week Ⓜ Moszkva tér, then 🚌 158

Sikló (Funicular)

Running between Clark Ádám tér and Buda Castle Palace. Re-opened in 1980, the ride lasts only two mins, but it is fun, especially for the youngest.

⊠ Terminus; Clark Ádám tér, Budapest ⏲ Daily 7:30–10. Closed Mon of every even-numbered week 🚌 16; Tram 19

Biking on Margaret Island

Margit-sziget (Margaret Island) is both safe and easy to ride around, and bikes and 'bike carriages' (available for hire on the island) are ideal for all the family. While there, the children might like to swim in the Palatinus pool or visit the mini-zoo.

Theatre, Opera, Dance & Music

Listings

Budapest has a vibrant nightlife with all types of activities and venues on offer. While visiting, pick up a copy of the English-language magazine *Budapest Week* for ideas. It carries extensive film, music, art and book reviews, plus listings of a wide range of venues and forthcoming events.

Theatre

Central Europe Dance Theatre

Folk and contemporary dance performances are held representing regional culture.

⊠ Bethlen Gábor tér 3, Budapest VII ☎ 342 7163

Merlin Theatre

Plays are performed in English by visiting and local groups, some performances in Hungarian.

⊠ Gerlóczy utca 4, Budapest V ☎ 317 9338

Operetta Theatre

The unrivalled venue for the best of Hungarian operetta and not to be missed.

⊠ Pest VI Nagymező utca 19 ☎ 332 0535

Petőfi Csarnok

City Park's excellent venue for theatre, arts and dance.

⊠ Zichy Mihály út 14, Budapest XIV ☎ 343 4327 Ⓜ Széchenyi Fürdő

Trafó House of Contemporary Art

Dance, drama and performance art by visiting groups, both local and abroad.

⊠ Liliom utca 41, Budapest IX ☎ 456 2040

Opera & Dance

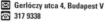

Erkel Színház (Erkel Theatre)

Not quite on the same scale as the State Opera, but always featuring an exciting programme with big names and lavish performances.

⊠ Köztársaság tér 30, Budapest VIII ☎ 333 0540 Ⓜ Blaha Lujza tér

Magyar Állami Operház (State Opera House)

World opera at one of the finest and most beautiful opera houses in Europe. Suitable for the *aficionado* and amateur alike (➤ 20).

⊠ Andrássy út 22, Budapest VI ☎ 3533 0170 Ⓜ M1 Opera

Folk Dancing

Fonó Music House

Regular folk dance with live bands where they teach you the dances of different regions and countries.

⊠ Sztregova utca 3, Budapest XI ☎ 206 6296

Kalamajka Club

Ideal for those who want to learn traditional Hungarian folk dance. Every Saturday evening.

⊠ District Cultural Centre, Molnár utca 9, Budapest V ☎ 317 5928

Church Music

Mátyás-templom (Matthais Church)

Choral and orchestral music can be enjoyed regularly at one of Budapest's finest churches, with concerts generally every Sunday afternoon at 2. Excellent acoustics.

⊠ Szentháromság tér 2, Budapest V ☎ 355 5657 🚌 16; Varbusz

Szent István Bazilika (St Stephen's Basilica)

Evening performances (usually beginning at 7) of classical, choral and orchestral music in this richly decorated and ornate church.

⊠ Szent István tér 1, Budapest I ☎ 411 0839 Ⓜ M3 Arany János utca

Cafés, Bars & Clubs

Cafés

Calgary
This tiny bar and antiques shop is a good place for conversation. It features a wide range of beers and frequent live piano music.
✉ **Frankel Leo út 24, Budapest II** ☎ **315 0045**

Gerbeaud
Considered to be the largest and most popular coffee house in the city, it offers a fine selection of pastries.
✉ **Vörösmary tér 7, Budapest V** ☎ **318 1311**

Lukács
One of the old-time cafés, recently renovated.
✉ **Andrássy út 70, Budapest VI** ☎ **302 8747**

Old Amsterdam
As with most Dutch places, this bar offers a excellent selection of imported beers.
✉ **Király Pál utca 14, Budapest V** ☎ **266 3649**

Ruszwurm
Claims to be the city's oldest existing café; located in the Castle district. Excellent cakes that can be eaten here or taken away.
✉ **Szentháromság utca, Budapest I** ☎ **375 5284**

Nightclubs & Bars

Angel Bar
Smart upstairs and rustic downstairs, this gay venue features a transvestite show on Friday and Sunday.
✉ **Szövétseg ut 33, Budapest VII**

Bahnhof
Bahnhof is a big club with railroad theme. It has two dance floors for rock and disco (no techno), and frequent live acts. Serves draught Belgian and Czech beers. Cover charge.
✉ **Váci út 1, Budapest VI** ☎ **302 8599** ◷ **Wed–Sat 9PM–4AM** 🚇 **Nyugati**

Bamboo Club
A tropical-theme bar with ersatz climate, playing boogie, 1970s disco, funk and soul. Cover charge.
✉ **Dessewffy utca 44, Budapest VI** ☎ **312 3619** ◷ **Mon–Fri 3PM–dawn, Sat, Sun from 7PM**

Beckett's
This great Irish-style pub serves good grub and beer. Frequented by home-sick expats. It was voted 'Best Bar 1996' by *Budapest Week*.
✉ **V, Bajcsy–Zsilinszky ut. 72** ☎ **311 1035** ◷ **Daily 12 till late**

Benczúr Club
A good small club for serious music fans without much money. Features live music Wednesday to Sunday after 7PM. Wednesday it's jazz; Thursday to Saturday live blues, rock and alternative; Sunday classical. Cover charge.
✉ **Benczúr utca 27, Budapest VI** ☎ **321 7334**

Black Rouge Night & Dance Club
Here you'll find Dionysian danseuses whose scantily dressed bodies writhe erotically to seduce you and your wallet. Entry is free, but don't ask for a drinks price list.
✉ **Hegyalja út 2, Budapest I** ☎ **381 0061**

If Your Face Doesn't Fit
Nowadays it seems that every western bar, pub and disco employs increasingly fussy doormen (bouncers to you and me) who like nothing more than to ruin your evening at a whim. But usually, unless you are obviously drunk or causing trouble, they will leave you alone. Not in Budapest though, where the bouncers are not to be tangled with, spoken to or upset in any way if you know what's good for you.

At the Cinema

Budapest has over 40 cinemas and art theatres showing all the top commercial films in English and some of the best Hungarian films on release with English subtitles. During the summer months something of a film fest takes place in Budapest showing many recent Hungarian film classics like *Confrontation*, *The Witness*, *The Whistling Cobblestone* and *Little Valentino* (very revealing about Budapest itself) being shown. A comprehensive film listing and guide is included in the English-language newspaper *Budapest Sun*.

Caligula Night Club

Here you'll find the 'pleasure principle' at sobering prices. Before you've even sat down with a small beer you will have parted with a sizeable amount of your money.

✉ Szilágyi Erzsébet fasor 37–39, Budapest II ☎ 212 3177

Capital AC/DC Singles Bar

A gay and mixed bar with occasional live shows and home-brewed beer. Free admission.

✉ Verseny utca 2, Budapest VII ☎ 352 1457 🕐 Mon–Sat 10PM–5AM. Closed Sun

Club Seven

This café, bar and music club is located on different levels with good jazz performances on the middle level.

✉ Akácfa utca 7, Budapest VII ☎ 478 9030 🕐 10AM–5PM

Crazy Café

The Crazy Café features karaoke, mainstream music, washed down with expensive German beer or Guinness. A large menu is also on offer.

✉ V, Jókai utca 30 ☎ 302 3969

E–Klub

Despite a jaded ambience, there are good live acts in the main hall with mixed music and various DJs on the dance floors.

✉ Népliget, Budapest X ☎ 263 1614 🕐 Fri, Sat 8–5am

Face

Located in the Nyugati station complex, house and techno music compete here with raunchy day-glo gyrations.

✉ Teréz korut 55, Budapest VI

☎ 44 5025 🕐 Thu–Sun 9PM–5AM

Fat Mo's

The weekend sees this elaborately furnished bar, awith prohibition era theme, packed with visitors and executives. Its attractions are affordable Irish beers, decent live bands and dancing.

✉ Nyári Pál utca 11, Budapest V ☎ 267 3199 🕐 Daily 12–12

Fortuna

Located up on Castle Hill is this loud, slick and urbane restaurant/club that rocks till dawn.

✉ Hess András tér 4, Budapest I

Fregatt Pub

This was the city's first English-style pub and has a friendly atmosphere and an increasingly local crowd. Live bands are a frequent attraction.

✉ Molnár utca 26, Budapest V ☎ 318 9997 🕐 Daily 5–12

Globe Royal Mulató

On offer here is a 1930s-New York theme with a superb restaurant and unplugged blues or rock nightly, not forgetting the pool tables.

✉ Csemete utca 5, Budapest III ☎ 250 8930

High Life

This massive disco and cattle 'flesh' market is not really the sort of place for the shy, retiring type.

✉ Kalap ut 14, Budapest III ☎ 250 2979 🕐 Fri, Sat 10–7

Irish Cat Pub

This crowded but friendly bar

attracts a range of visitors and locals in search of Guinness and the occasional band.

✉ Múzeum körút 41, Budapest V ☎ 266 4085

John Bull Pub

This familiar chain of English-style pubs, with several outlets in Budapest and surroundings, is popular with business folk and visitors to the city. Among those in the city are Vadász and Víghajós.

✉ Podmaniczky tér, Budapest V; Budaörsi út 7, Budapest XI

Kisrablo Pub

This comfortable English-style pub serves acceptable food and Belgian beer.

✉ Zenta utca 3, Budapest XI ☎ 209 1588

Kőzgáz Jazz Club

With a good atmosphere, this is basically a student club with innovative jazz on Friday nights.

✉ Kinizsi utca 2–6, Budapest IX

The Long Jazz Club

This club features live music most nights; mainly traditional jazz.

✉ Dohány utca 22–24, Budapest VII ☎ 322 0006

Merlin Theatre/Club

Mostly a jazz and folk joint, with plenty of tables to take a reflective beer and relax. The club also serves some good food.

✉ Gerlóczy utca 4, Budapest V

Old Man's Music Pub

The interior may be designed like a faded living room, but on offer are nightly blues and folk, with good pizzas and other dishes featuring on the menu.

✉ Akácfa utca13, Budapest VII ☎ 322 7645 ⚫ Daily 3PM–dawn

Pesti Est Café

Located on Liszt Ferenc square off Anfrássy út, alongside all the other bars and cafés which have recently sprung up in the area. In summer it spills out into the square.

✉ Liszt Ferenc tér 5, Budapest VI ☎ 344 4382 ⚫ 11PM–2AM

Piaf

Named after the French singer, this basic club attracts a slightly more mature crowd.

✉ Nagymező u 25, Budapest VI ☎ 312 3823 ⚫ Daily 4–4

Shakal Club

This smart, new and expensive club with atrium and bistro plays house, funk and acid jazz form Thurday to Saturday. There is a cover charge.

✉ Apáczai Csere János utca 13, Budapest V ☎ 318 4677 ⚫ Daily 11PM–5AM

Tam Tam Club

This alcohol-free alternative club is part of a contemporary dance studio.

✉ Csanády utca 19, Budapest XIII ⚫ Daily 4PM–late, closed Sun

Trocadero Cafe

Spacious café with pool tables and dancing on separate levels. Hot Latin, Salsa bands pocket the best of the clientele, and even dance classes are on offer.

✉ Szent István körút 13, Budapest V ☎ 311 4691

Through the Night

In common with their counterparts in western capitals such as Amsterdam, Paris and Rome (not so much in London), some clubs and bars in Budapest open for a very long time. So gear up for a long day and evening, and bring plenty of money for partying.

Casinos & Sport

Taking the Waters
Throughout this guide there are a number of references to spas. However, they are just a fraction of the abundant medicinal and spring waters to be found in Budapest and the surrounding area. Hot springs on the Buda side of the river were used by the Celts and the Romans. There are 14 sources giving rise to over 120 thermal springs – of varying temperatures – and some 400 mineral springs.

Casinos
Casinos are popular in Budapest and most are concentrated in the Inner City. Below is just a selection of venues, offering an international choice of games in pleasant surroundings, with excellent service. Opening hours at these establishments tend to be extensive. The minimum gaming age is 18.

Budapest Hilton
Located on the sixth floor of the luxury Hilton Hotel, service is just as expected. Dress code: jacket and tie.
✉ **Hess András tér 1–3, Budapest I** ☎ **175 7001** 🕐 **Daily 7PM–2AM**

Las Vegas Casino
Well located at the foot of the Chain Bridge in Pest, within the Hyatt Regency Hotel. Free admission to the casino. Dess code: casual.
✉ **Roosevelt tér 2, Budapest V** ☎ **117 6022** 🕐 **Daily 2PM–5AM**

Tropicana
Tropicana offers baccarat and dice as well as the more familiar games.
✉ **Vigadó utca 2, Budapest V** ☎ **266 3062** 🕐 **Daily 2PM–5AM**

Várkert
Making a change from the hotel casinos is this stylish venue in the former pump-house designed for the Royal Palace. Admission is free. Dress code: casual.
✉ **Ybl Miklós tér, 9, Budapest I** ☎ **202 4244** 🕐 **Daily 2PM–5AM**

Sport

Billiards
You can play billiards in almost 100 venues around the city. Tables can be found mainly in pubs and clubs, but there are a few dedicated billiard halls, including:
Atlantis
✉ **Váci út 156, Budapest XIII**

Black Pool
✉ **Vámház körút 15, Budapest IX**

Noiret
✉ **Dessewffy utca 8–10, Budapest VI**

Vega
✉ **Árpád út 81, Budapest VI**

Bowling
As this pastime becomes increasingly widespread, two of the most popular of Budapest's bowling alleys can be found in the following hotels:
Novotel Budapest Centrum
✉ **Alkotás utca 63–77, Budapest XII**
☎ **286 9588**

Hotel Stadion
✉ **Ifjúság útja 1–3, Budapest XIV** ☎ **251 2222**

Canoeing
In its heyday of the 1950s the Danube was a popular spot for leisure boating. With its strong canoeing and kayaking traditions, Hungary plays host to a number of international competitions, generally held in Szeged.

Cycling
Budapest has few cycling paths and no dedicated network. Despite this, cycling is very popular but riding amongst the traffic is not advised. It is best to cycle in the large parks: Margit-sziget (Margaret Island), Városliget (City Park)

and Népliget (People's Park) where bikes are available for hire. More information can be found on cycling in *By Bike in Budapest*, available from local tourist information offices.

Flying

Weather permitting, there are a number of options available, both for pleasure flights and for qualified amateurs to pilot their own craft. Small planes can also be chartered for excursions to the Danube Bend. Flights are usually possible daily between 8AM and sunset, lasting a minimum of 10 minutes. Pleasure flights, hang-gliding and gliding are available from Budakeszi-Farkas-hegy Airport, 5km west of the city, and pleasure flights from Budaörs Airport (1.5km south). It is best to book in advance.

Budakeszi-Farkas-hegy Airport
☎ (23) 450 694

Budaörs Airport
✉ Köérberki út 36 ☎ 249 9826

Golf

The nearest golf course is the excellent Budapest Golf Park & Country Club at Kisoroszi on the Danube Bend, 35km north of Budapest – an 18-hole course where you can hire equipment. Tennis courts are also available. Advance booking only.
☎ 318 8030

Horse-riding

Hungarians have a tradition of horsemanship and two places worth considering for riding are Budapest Equestrian Club and Petneházy Horse-Riding School:
✉ **Kerepesi út 7, Budapest VIII**
☎ **313 8679**

✉ **Feketefej ut 2–4, Budapest II**
☎ **397 5048**

Hot-air Ballooning

Flights for at least two people lasting a minimum of one hour are available daily in the morning and evening, weather permitting. A minibus will take participants to and from the take-off spot. Bookings are necessary.
Sup-Air Balloon Club
☎ 322 0015

Motor racing

The major event of each year is the Hungarian Formula One Grand Prix held each August at the Hungaroring, off the motorway about 20km east of Budapest. From spring to late autumn, budding racers can also enter dragster-style races. Registrations are accepted on the day; bring your own car, a valid driving licence and registration documents – and a lot of nerve.

Rowing

Boats are available for hire on Margaret Island (✉ Danubius Nemzeti Hajós Egylet, Hajós Alfred Pool). Boathouses along the Romai Bank also have boats for hire.

Tennis

There are many courts for hire throughout the city. The Hungarian Tennis Association has full details:
✉ **Dósza György út 1–3, Budapest XIV** ☎ **252 6687**

115

What's On When

Check Before You Go

As many of these festivities have movable dates, it is always a good idea to check with the tourist information offices and in local publications such as *Budapest Sun* before attending. Also, don't forget that accommodation can be snapped up a long time in advance of festivals, events and public holidays.

January

1 January: New Year Opera Gala, Budapest.

March

Budapest Spring Festival: First-class concerts, opera, dance, theatre and folklore performances as well as master classes and exhibitions at several venues in the city.

April

March/April: *Easter Festival* in Hollókő including an open-air service and food blessing. Book of Grapes Coming, a traditional festival predicting the expected grape harvest, Kőszeg.

May

Balaton Festival in Keszthely opens with the laying of a wreath on Lake Balaton, the 'Hungarian Sea.'
International Dixieland Festival in Salgótarján.

June

World Music Festival.
Földvár Festival (Balatönföldvár) including running contests, fireworks and local art ensembles.
Pécs: The town's summer festival kicks off with concerts and displays of ethnic folklore.
Sopron: Dance and music to start the summer festival.

July

International Danube Cruise when Hungary and the world take to the Danube in a variety of crafts.
Budapest's International Jazz Festival:
start of a series of open-air concerts and theatrical performances on Margaret Island. Also concerts in the Domincan Courtyard of the Hilton Hotel.
Medieval games in Visegrád Palace, with jousting and tournaments.
International Folk Festival, Siófok.
Balaton Folk Art Meeting with Hungarian and foreign dance ensembles.
Over 5km swim across Lake Balaton.

August

The Hungarian Formula One Grand Prix: usually takes place on the second Sunday of the month at the Hungaroring motor-racing circuit, about 20k outside Budapest.
BudaFest Summer Opera and Ballet Festival. Held at the State Opera House (▶ 20).
St Stephen's Day: Countrywide celebrations with processions, fireworks.

September

Budapest International Ballet Contest:
International stars in the Opera and International Ballet Gala for Children.
Budapest International Wine Festival.
Music weeks (or may start in October)

October

Budapest Autumn Festival: Concerts, theatre, ballet, film and art exhibitions (starting late September).
Public holiday commemorating 1956 Revolution.

December

Christmas fairs held in several parts of the city. New Year's Eve Gala and Ball, Budapest.

Practical
Matters

Above: *friendly faces on the
streets of Budapest*
Right: *one of many imposing
statues in the city*

GMT	Budapest	Germany	USA (NY)	Netherlands	Spain
12 noon	→1PM	→1PM	←7AM	→1PM	→1PM

BEFORE YOU GO

WHAT YOU NEED

- ● Required
- ○ Suggested
- ▲ Not required

	UK	Germany	USA	Netherlands	Spain
Passport/National Identity Card	●	●	●	●	●
Visa	▲	▲	▲	▲	▲
Onward or Return Ticket	●	●	●	●	●
Health Inoculations	▲	▲	▲	▲	▲
Health Documentation (Reciprocal Agreement Document, ➤ 123, Health)	●	▲	▲	▲	▲
Travel Insurance	○	○	○	○	○
Driving Licence (National or International)	●	●	●	●	●
Car Insurance Certificate (if own car)	●	●	●	●	●
Car registration document (if own car)	●	●	●	●	●

WHEN TO GO

Budapest

High season
Low season

JAN	FEB	MAR	APR	MAY	JUN	JUL	AUG	SEP	OCT	NOV	DEC
0°C	0°C	10°C	18°C	22°C	25°C	28°C	26°C	24°C	16°C	8°C	0°C

Wet   Cloud   Sun   Sunshine/showers

TOURIST OFFICES

In the UK
Hungarian National Tourist Board
PO Box 4336
London SW18 4XE
24hr Information: ☎ (0891) 171 200;
fax: (0891) 669 970
☎ Fax (0181) 871 4009
(Administration)

In the USA
Hungarian Tourist Board
c/o Embassy of the Republic of Hungary
Office of the Commercial Counsellor
150 East 58th Street 33rd floor
New York
NY 10155
☎ 212/355 0240; fax 212/207 4103

POLICE 107

FIRE 105

AMBULANCE 104

WHEN YOU ARE THERE

ARRIVING

The national airline, Malév ☎ (1) 266 5616/266 5050 operates scheduled flights to Budapest's Ferihegy Airport from major European cities. Budapest has three international railway stations: Keleti (Eastern), Nyugati (Western) and Déli (Southern); for rail travel from the UK contact Rail Europe ☎ (0990) 300003.

Budapest, Ferihegy Airport, Kilometres to city centre	Journey times
	🚆 N/A
	🚌 Minibus 40 minutes
20/24 kilometres	🚗 30 minutes

Keleti, Nyugati and Déli Stations Kilometres to city centre	Journey times
	🚆 few stops on metro
	🚌 Rail-bus service
1–5 kilometres	🚗 N/A

MONEY

The monetary unit of Hungary is the forint (HUF), subdivided into 100 worthless fillérs. Coins are in denominations of 1, 2, 5, 10, 20, 50, 100 and 200 forints. Most purchases involve the use of banknotes, which come in denominations of 100, 500,1,000, 5,000, 10,000 and 20,000 forints.
Travellers' cheques and convertible currency can be changed in banks, post offices, travel offices and hotels, and credit cards are in increasing use, but by no means everywhere. Eurocheques may be used up to a limit of 30,000 forints.

TIME

Hungary is on Central European Time, one hour ahead of Greenwich Mean Time (GMT+1), but from early March to late October, daylight saving (GMT+2) operates.

CUSTOMS

→ **YES**

The following may be imported duty free into Hungary by persons over the age of 16.

Alcohol: spirits: 1L *and*
Wine: 2L *and*
Beer: 5L
Cigarettes: 500 *or*
Cigars: 100 *or*
Tobacco: 500gms *or*
Perfume and toilet water: 'reasonable' amount
Tea, coffee, cocoa: 1kg
Goods to a value of 21,000 forints can be bought in duty free on one occasion a year. No more than 300,000 forints in Hungarian currency per person may be brought in to Hungary.

⊖ **NO**

Obscene material, narcotics, explosives, firearms, ammunition and pure alcohol.

UK	Germany	USA	Netherlands	Spain
(1) 266 2888	(1) 467 3500	(1) 267 4400	(1) 326 5301	(1) 342 9933

WHEN YOU ARE THERE

TOURIST OFFICES

National Tourist Information Centre (Tourinform)

● Sütő utca 2, Budapest V (near Deák tér Metro Station)
☎ 438 8080
Fax: 356 1964
E-mail: hungary@tourinform.hu

also at:

● Vörösmarty tér (corner of Vigadó u) 0–24

Tourism Office of Budapest

In writing:

● 1364 Budapest, POB 215
Fax: 266 0497

In person:

● Nyugati Railway Station Main Concourse
☎ Fax: 302 8580

● Budaörs, Agip–Complex (M7–M1 motorways)
☎ (23) 417 518

Touchscreen Information (Info Touch)

● Tourinform offices
● Ferihegy Airport
● Déli Railway Station
● Astoria Metro Station
● Grand Market Hall
● Hungarian Culture Foundation (Szentháromság tér 6)

NATIONAL HOLIDAYS

J	F	M	A	M	J	J	A	S	O	N	D
1		1(2)	(1)	1	1		1		1		2

1 Jan:	New Year's Day
15 Mar:	Anniversary of 1848–9 Revolution
Mar/Apr:	Easter Monday
1 May:	Labour Day
May/Jun:	Whit Monday
20 Aug:	St Stephen's Day
23 Oct:	Anniversary of 1956 Revolution
25 Dec:	Christmas Day
26 Dec:	Boxing Day

In Hungary most offices, shops and other facilities close down on public holidays and, should any of these holidays be on a Tuesday or Thursday, the day between it and the weekend also becomes a public holiday.

OPENING HOURS

○ Shops ● Post Offices
● Offices ◐ Museums/Monuments
● Banks ◐ Pharmacies

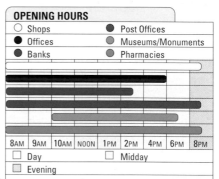

8AM	9AM	10AM	NOON	1PM	2PM	4PM	6PM	8PM

☐ Day ☐ Midday
☐ Evening

Saturday afternoon is early closing and few shops remain open after 1PM. Thursday is late-night shopping (until 7 or 8). Supermarkets and other food shops have longer hours and are open Sunday mornings. In large centres some shops open 24 hours. In smaller places shops often close for lunch. Pharmacies follow shop hours but there is always one open late in each area. Banks have early closing (1PM) on Fridays.

The majority of museums are closed Monday; in winter they usually close earlier. Large churches are open throughout the day, in small towns and villages they may only open early morning and/or evening (6–9PM).

**DRIVE ON THE
RIGHT**

**TOILETS
CHARGE**

★★
★★

PUBLIC TRANSPORT

Trains: Metro A comprehensive system covers most of the city. Lines are colour-coded. Yellow line (M1): Vörösmarty tér to Mexikói út. Red line (M2): east of city to the centre of Moszkva tér and to the Déli Railway Station. Blue line (M3): southeast to the downtown area to the northern part of the city. Tickets are available at stations until 8PM at the regular *pénztár* (counter), after this time you can get them from the section called *forgalmi ügyelet*. You must validate your ticket at the orange machine otherwise the police may be called and a fine imposed. Trains operate from 4:30AM to 11:10PM.

Buses There are more than 200 bus routes in the capital. Bus numbers in red which are followed by a red letter E are non-stop express buses, stopping only at the two termini. Buses with red-and-black numbers not suffixed with E are the normal buses. Tickets are bought from newsagents or in the underground. Hotels occasionally sell them.

River Boats A scheduled passenger-boat service operates on the Danube from May to August (Thursday to Sunday), 9AM to 5PM). The route is Boráros tér to Rómaifürdő with frequent stops in between. You can embark or disembark at any point – timetables are displayed.

Urban Transport: Trams There is a wide network of trams in the city with frequent stations. As with the bus, tickets have to be bought in the metro or at newsagents.
Trolleybuses Currently there are 15 routes. You can travel on trolleybuses with tram tickets.
HÉV Surburban Trains These serve Budapest and its environs. Yellow signs indicate departures, white ones indicate arrivals.

CAR RENTAL

International car-hire firms have arrangements with local travel agencies, and hire cars are available through them. Avis, is linked with Ibusz, whose 90 offices cover the whole country. The driver must be over 21 and have held a licence for more than one year.

TAXIS

Be careful of rogue taxis that do not display signs. Recommended are:
Budataxi ☎ 233 3333;
Citytaxi ☎ 211 1111;
Főtaxi ☎ 222 2222;
6x6 ☎ 266 6666;
Rádiotaxi ☎ 277 7777;
Volantaxi ☎ 266 6666.

DRIVING

Speed limit on motorways: **130kph**

Speed limit on major roads: **100kph**
Other roads: **90kph**
Cars with trailers, coaches: **70kph**

Speed limit in built-up areas: **50kph**

Seat belts must be worn in front seats and rear seats where fitted.

There is a total alcohol ban for drivers in Hungary.

Petrol (leaded and unleaded) is readily available. Opening times vary, but there are 24-hour stations. Self-service is the norm. Credit cards are not accepted everywhere.

Contact the Hungarian Automobile Association (☎ 212 2821, 24-hour service) which is affiliated to the AA. In the case of an accident call the police (☎ 107) in the first instance. Assistance with insurance can be obtained from the Hungaria Insurance Company,1113 Budapest, Hamzsabégi út 60 ☎ 209 0730. Vehicles with damaged bodywork may only leave the country with an official certificate.

PERSONAL SAFETY

Security is no worse than in any other foreign capital. The most frequent crimes are pickpocketing, confidence tricks and car theft. Tourist Police and uniformed guards, accompanied by interpreters, patrol main tourist areas from July to August.

- Avoid street vendors and beggars.
- Beware of attractive offers.
- Don't carry too much cash.
- Never leave valuables in your car.
- Victims of crime should contact the Tourist Police, Vigadóu 6, Budapest V (24 hours) or ☎ 438 8080

Police assistance:
☎ **107** from any call box

TELEPHONES

Coin and card telephones are widely available. Coin phones accept 20, 50, 100 forint coins. Phonecards can be bought in 50 and 120 units for 800 forints and 1,800 forints respectively. Phonecards can be bought at hotels, newsagents, petrol stations, tobacconists and post offices. For local calls, dial the number required. For inland calls dial 06, the area code, followed by the subscriber's number. For international calls, dial 00, the country access code, the area code (minus any initial '0'), and finally the subscriber's number.

International Dialling Codes	
From Hungary to:	
UK:	**00 44**
Germany:	**00 49**
USA:	**00 1**
Netherlands:	**00 31**
Spain:	**00 34**

POST

There are two 24-hour, seven-day, post offices: at Nyugati Railway Station, Teréz körút 51-3; also at

Keleti Railway Station, Baross tér 11/c. Otherwise, post offices are open Mon–Fri 8–6; Sat 8–2. *Poste restante* mail can be collected from the post office at Városház utca 18. Stamps can also be bought at tobacconist shops (*bélyeg*) and in hotels.

ELECTRICITY

The power supply is 220 volts AC. Sockets accept two-pin round plugs, so an adaptor is needed for most non-continental European appliances, and a transformer for appliances operating on 100–120 volts.

TIPS/GRATUITIES

Yes ✓ No ✗		
Hotels (if service not included)	✓	10 %
Restaurants (if service not included)	✓	10–20%
Cafés/bars	✓	10%
Taxis	✓	10%
Hairdressers	✓	10–15%
Usherettes	✓	change
Cloakroom attendants	✓	change
Toilets	✓	change
Garage attendants	✓	change

HEALTH

Insurance
All visitors to Hungary receive free first aid and transport to hospital. However, there is a charge for all other treatment so it is essential to take out comprehensive health insurance.

Dental Services
Dental treatment and associated prescribed medicines must be paid for. High-quality dental work is relatively inexpensive by western standards. Contact your embassy for details of dentists speaking foreign languages.

Sun Advice
During the high season temperatures can rise into the 30°C with bright sunshine. It is recommended that you wear a sunhat and cover the skin as Budapest can receive around nine hours of sunshine in July and August.

Drugs
Pharmacies (*gyógyszertár* or *patika*) issue a wide range of drugs, but mostly originating in Eastern European. If you require special medication you should take it with you. Products tend to be cheaper than in the West.

Safe Water
Tap water is safe to drink. Otherwise, bottled water is widely available if you prefer. Look for *ásvány víz* (mineral water) or *szóda víz* (soda water).

CONCESSIONS

Students/Youths
Holders of an International Student Identity Card (ISIC) can take advantage of reductions at hostels and campsites, and generous discounts on trains and Malév flights. Vista, Váciút 19/b, Budapest XIII ☎ 237 5010, provides information on all student discounts and opportunities in Hungary.

Senior Citizens
Senior citizens with Rail Europe Senior Cards can claim a reduction on train fares.

CLOTHING SIZES

Hungary	UK	Rest of Europe	USA	
46	36	46	36	
48	38	48	38	
50	40	50	40	
52	42	52	42	
54	44	54	44	
56	46	56	46	Suits
41	7	41	8	
42	7.5	42	8.5	
43	8.5	43	9.5	
44	9.5	44	10.5	
45	10.5	45	11.5	
46	11	46	12	Shoes
37	14.5	37	14.5	
38	15	38	15	
39/40	15.5	39/40	15.5	
41	16	41	16	
42	16.5	42	16.5	
43	17	43	17	Shirts
36	8	34	6	
38	10	36	8	
40	12	38	10	
42	14	40	12	
44	16	42	14	
46	18	44	16	Dresses
38	4.5	38	6	
38	5	38	6.5	
39	5.5	39	7	
39	6	39	7.5	
40	6.5	40	8	
41	7	41	8.5	Shoes

WHEN DEPARTING

- Contact the airport or travel representative 72 hours prior to departing to ensure flight details are unchanged.
- Arrive 90 minutes before your scheduled flight departure time (especially during summer) or you may miss your flight.
- Departing visitors must have a boarding card (collected at check-in desks) to present at passport control.

LANGUAGE

Hungarian (Magyar) belongs to the Finno-Ugric group and lies outside the mainstream of European languages. While its spellings are logical, understanding and speaking it pose considerable difficulties to foreigners. Guesswork and improvisation can lead to considerable confusion. English is gradually replacing German as the principal second language, especially among the young. Locals in service industries usually speak German and/or English, and hotel staff may understand several languages.

hotel	szálloda	reservation	foglalás
room	szoba	rate	szobaár
single/	egyágyas/	breakfast	regbeli
double	francia ágyas	toilet/bathroom	WC/fürdőszoba
one/two nights	egy/	shower	zuhany
	kettő ejszakdra	balcony	erkély
per person/	egy személyre/	reception	recepció
per room	egy szoba ára	key	kulcs

bank	bank	US dollar	dollár
exchange office	pénzváltó	banknote	bankjegy
post office	posta	coin	érme
cashier	pénztáros	credit card	hitelkártya
foreign	külföldi deviza	cheque book	csekk-kőnyv
exchange		exchange rate	árfolyam
foreign currency	külföldi valuta	commission	pénzváltási
pound sterling	font	charge	jutalék

restaurant	étterem	starter	előétel
café	kávéház	main course	főétel
table	asztal	dish of the day	napi ajánlat
menu	menükartya	dessert	édesség
set menu	menu	the bill	számla
wine list	bor lista	drink	ital
lunch	ebéd	waiter	pincér
dinner	vacsora	waitress	pincérnő

aeroplane	repülőgép	first/second	első/
airport	repülőtér	class	másodosztályő
train	vonat	ticket office	jegy pénztár
station	állomás	timetable	menetrend
bus station	busz allomás	seat	ülőhely
ferry terminal	komp kikőtő	non-smoking	nem dománYZó
ticket	jegy	reserved	foglalt
single/return	egyirányú/retur	departure	indulás

do you speak English?	beszél angolul?	thank you	köszönöm
I don't under-stand	nem értem	excuse me	elnézést
		do you know where...is?	tudja merre van a...
yes	igen	to the right/left	jobbra/balra
no/not	nem	straight on	egyenesen
good morning/ night	jó regggel/ éjszakát	many/much	sok
		little/few	kevés
goodbye	viszontlátásra	expensive	drága
please	kérem	cheap	olcsó

INDEX

Acknowledgements

The Automobile Assocation wishes to thank the following photographers, libraries and associations for their assistance in the preparation of this book:

The Automobile Association wishes to thank the following photographers, libraries and associations for their assistance in the preparation of this book.

ROBERT HARDING PICTURE LIBRARY 70b, 85; **HULTON GETTY** 11b; **HUNGARIAN NATIONAL GALLERY** 41c; **HUNGARIAN NATIONAL MUSEUM** 66b; **MRI BANKER'S GUIDE TO FOREIGN CURRENCY** 119; **MUSEUM OF CONTEMPORARY ART – LUDWIG COLLECTION** 41b; **NATIONAL SZÉCHÉNYI LIBRARY** 45b; **NATURE PHOTOGRAPHERS LTD** 13b (R I Smith)

All remaining photographs are held in the Association's own library (**AA Photo Library**) and were taken by Ken Paterson with the exception of the following:
E Meacher F/cover a (horse), d (hedgehog sign), e (Fisherman's Bastion), bottom (carving), 5a, 6a, 7a, 8a, 9a, 10a, 11a, 12a, 13a, 14a, 15b, 19b, 20b, 21b, 22b, 29b, 31b, 35, 37, 38c, 47b, 49, 57b, 58c, 60/1, 69, 76b, 80, 81, 86b, 89, 90b; **P Wilson** 12b, 18b, 32b, 36b, 56b, 63c; **G Wrona** B/cover, 8c, 23b, 83b, 84b, 122a, 122b.

Copy editor: Colin Follett   **Page layout**: Jo Tapper

Dear Essential Traveller

Your comments, opinions and recommendations are very important to us. So please help us to improve our travel guides by taking a few minutes to complete this simple questionnaire.

You do not need a stamp (unless posted outside the UK). If you do not want to cut this page from your guide, then photocopy it or write your answers on a plain sheet of paper.

Send to: **The Editor, AA World Travel Guides, FREEPOST SCE 4598, Basingstoke RG21 4GY.**

Your recommendations...

We always encourage readers' recommendations for restaurants, nightlife or shopping – if your recommendation is used in the next edition of the guide, we will send you a *FREE* AA *Essential* **Guide** of your choice. Please state below the establishment name, location and your reasons for recommending it.

_____

_____

_____

_____

Please send me **AA *Essential*** _____

(*see list of titles inside the front cover*)

About this guide...

Which title did you buy?

AA *Essential* _____

Where did you buy it? _____

When? m m / y y

Why did you choose an AA *Essential* Guide? _____

_____

_____

_____

_____

Did this guide meet your expectations?

Exceeded ☐ Met all ☐ Met most ☐ Fell below ☐

Please give your reasons _____

_____

_____

_____

continued on next page...

Were there any aspects of this guide that you particularly liked? _____

_____

_____

_____

Is there anything we could have done better? _____

_____

_____

_____

_____

About you...

Name (*Mr/Mrs/Ms*) _____

    Address _____

_____

_____ Postcode _____

    Daytime tel nos _____

Which age group are you in?

    Under 25 ☐   25–34 ☐   35–44 ☐   45–54 ☐   55–64 ☐   65+ ☐

How many trips do you make a year?

    Less than one ☐   One ☐   Two ☐   Three or more ☐

Are you an AA member? Yes ☐   No ☐

About your trip...

When did you book? m m / y y   When did you travel? m m / y y

How long did you stay? _____

Was it for business or leisure? _____

Did you buy any other travel guides for your trip?

    If yes, which ones? _____

_____

Thank you for taking the time to complete this questionnaire. Please send it to us as soon as possible, and remember, you do not need a stamp (*unless posted outside the UK*).

Happy Holidays!